Maria D

CROSS STITCH MOTIF SERIES 1
KANAVİÇE MOTİF SERİSİ 1

GARDEN & FLOWERS
BAHÇE VE ÇİÇEKLER

200 NEW CROSS STITCH MOTIFS
200 YENİ KANAVİÇE MOTİFİ

Tuva Yayıncılık / Tuva Publishing
www.tuvayayincilik.com

Adres / Address: Merkez Mah. Çavuşbaşı Cad. No:71
Çekmeköy / - İstanbul 34782 / Turkey
Tel: 9 0216 642 62 62

Kanaviçe Motif Serisi 1 / Bahçe ve Çiçekler
Cross Sttich Motif Series 1 / Garden & Flower

İlk Basım / First Print: 2011 / Ekim - October, Istanbul
İkinci Basım / Second Print: 2012 / Kasım - November, Istanbul
Üçüncü Basım / Third Print: 2013 /Mayıs - May - Istanbul

Konusu / Content: Kanaviçe - Cross Stitch

Yayın Yönetmeni / Editor in Chief: Ayhan DEMİRPEHLİVAN
Proje Editörü / Project Editor: Kader DEMİRPEHLİVAN
Tasarımcı / Designer: Maria DIAZ
Teknik Danışman / Technical Advisor: K. Leyla ARAS
Grafik / Graphic Design: Ömer ALP, Büşra ESER
Asistan / Asistant: Kevser BAYRAKÇI

ISBN: 978-605-5647-23-0

Basıldığı Matbaa / Printing House
Bilnet Matbaacılık - Biltur Yayın ve Hizmet A.Ş. Dudullu
Organize Sanayi Bölgesi 1. Cadde No:16 - Ümraniye - İstanbul / Turkey
Tel: 9 0216 444 44 03

1
2
3
4
5
6
7
8
9
10
11
12
13
14
15
16
17
18
19
20
21
22
23
24
25
26
27

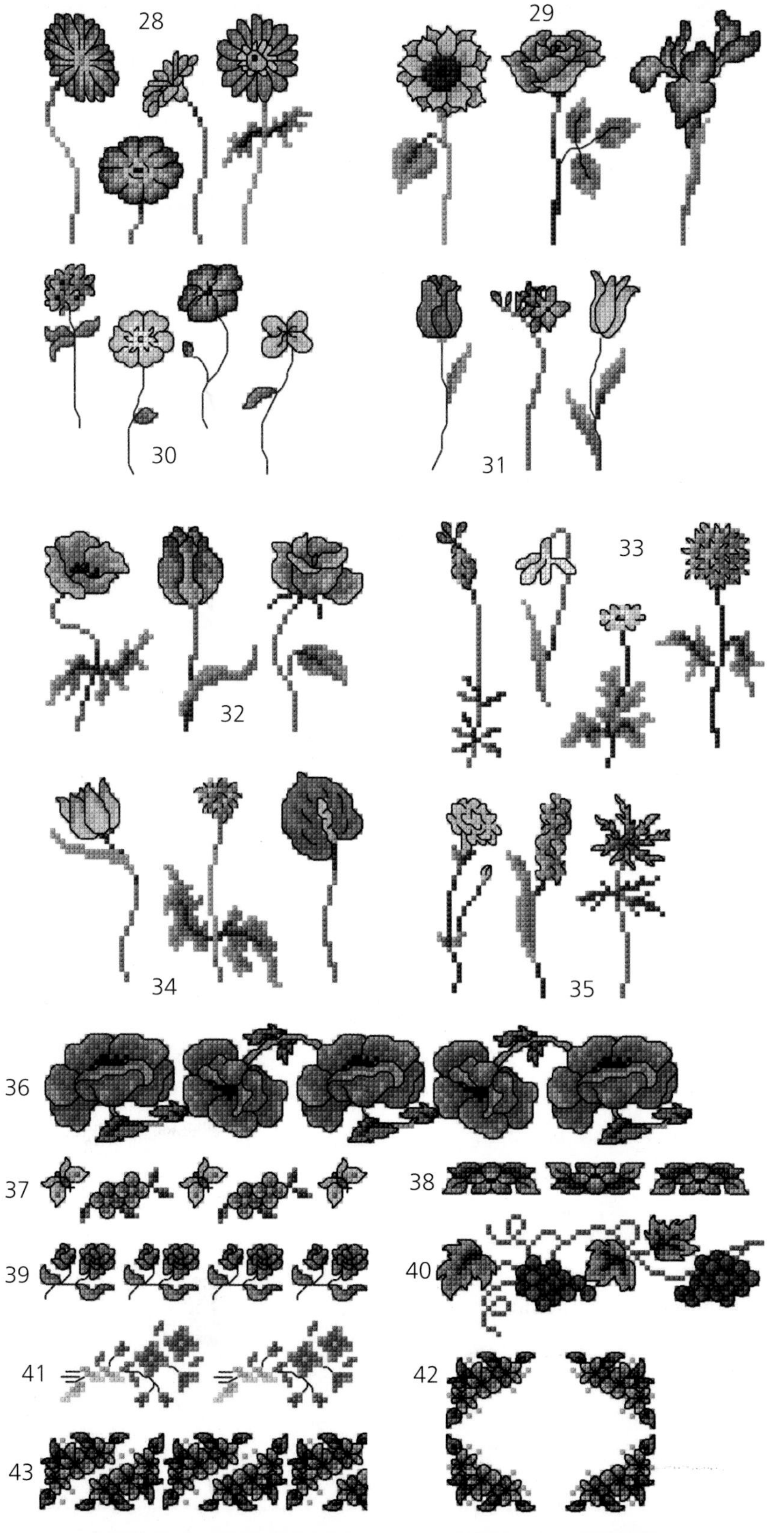
28
29
30
31
32
33
34
35
36
37
38
39
40
41
42
43

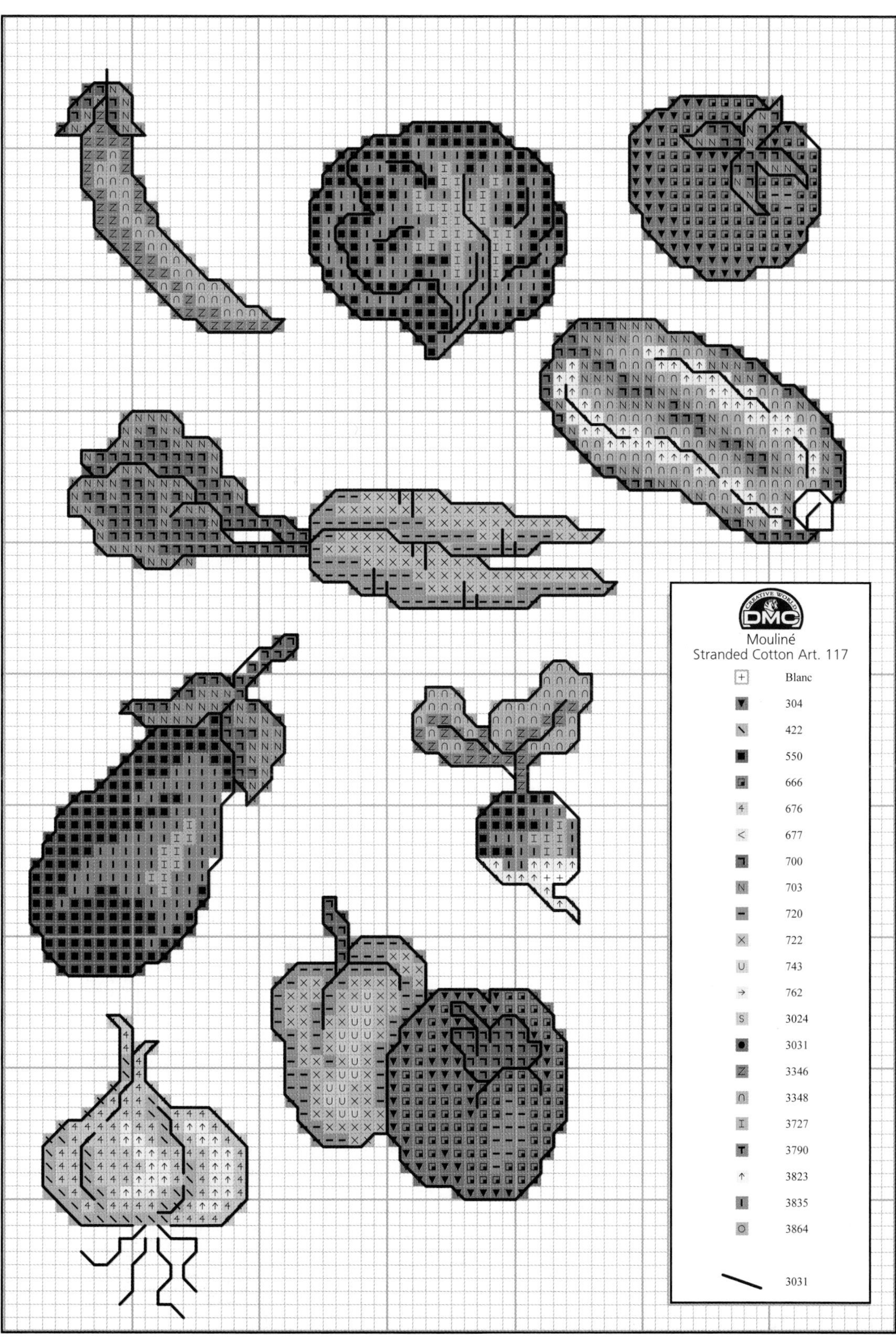
DMC
CREATIVE WORLD
Mouliné
Stranded Cotton Art. 117
Blanc
304
422
550
666
676
677
700
703
720
722
743
762
3024
3031
3346
3348
3727
3790
3823
3835
3864
3031

DMC
CREATIVE WORLD
Mouliné
Stranded Cotton Art. 117
Blanc
597
601
603
605
699
703
726
742
819
939
947
3078
3809
939

CREATIVE WORLD
DMC
Mouliné
Stranded Cotton Art. 117
210
340
355
367
368
472
712
725
727
961
3024
3345
3347
844
3716
3746
3771
3774
3813
355
844

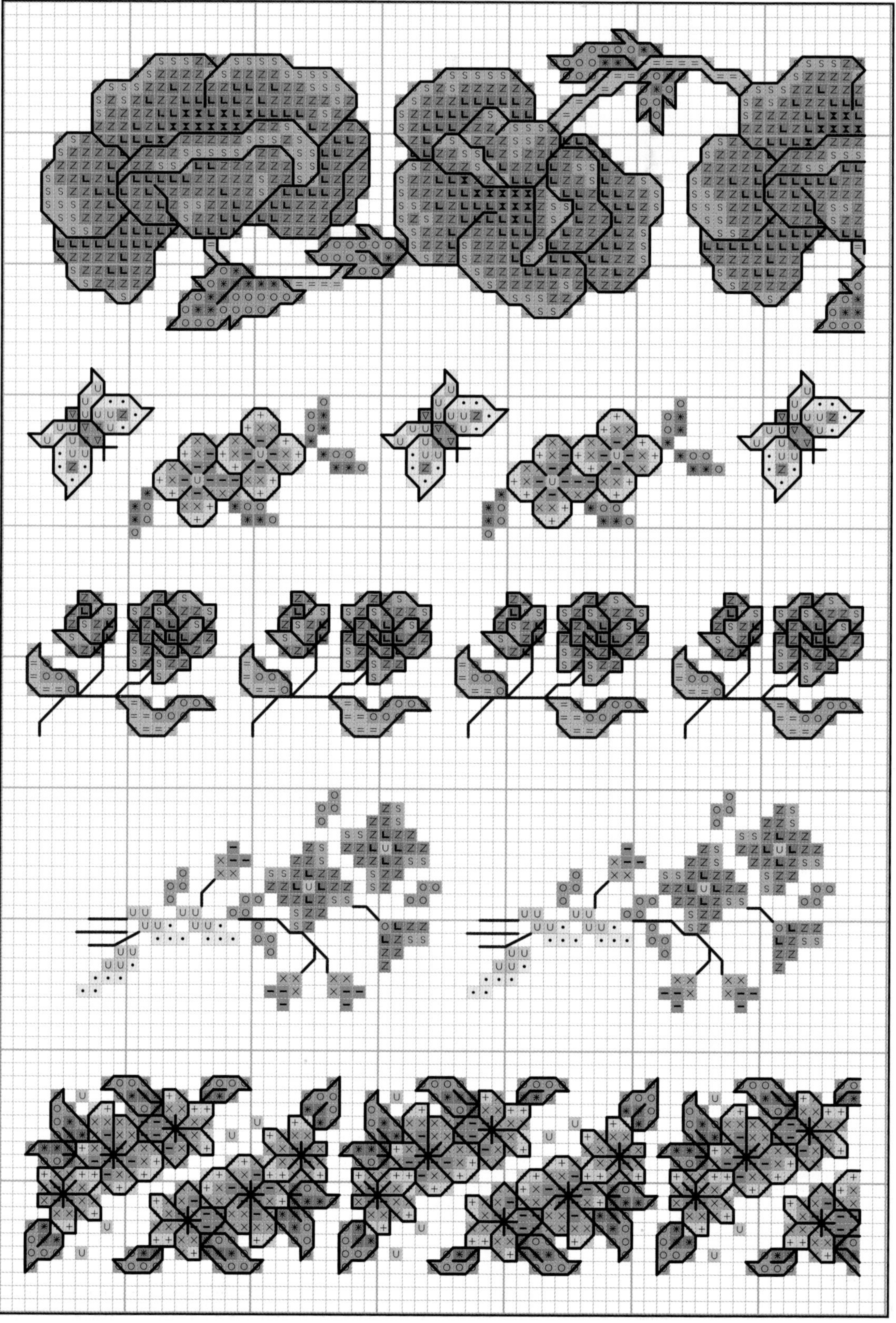

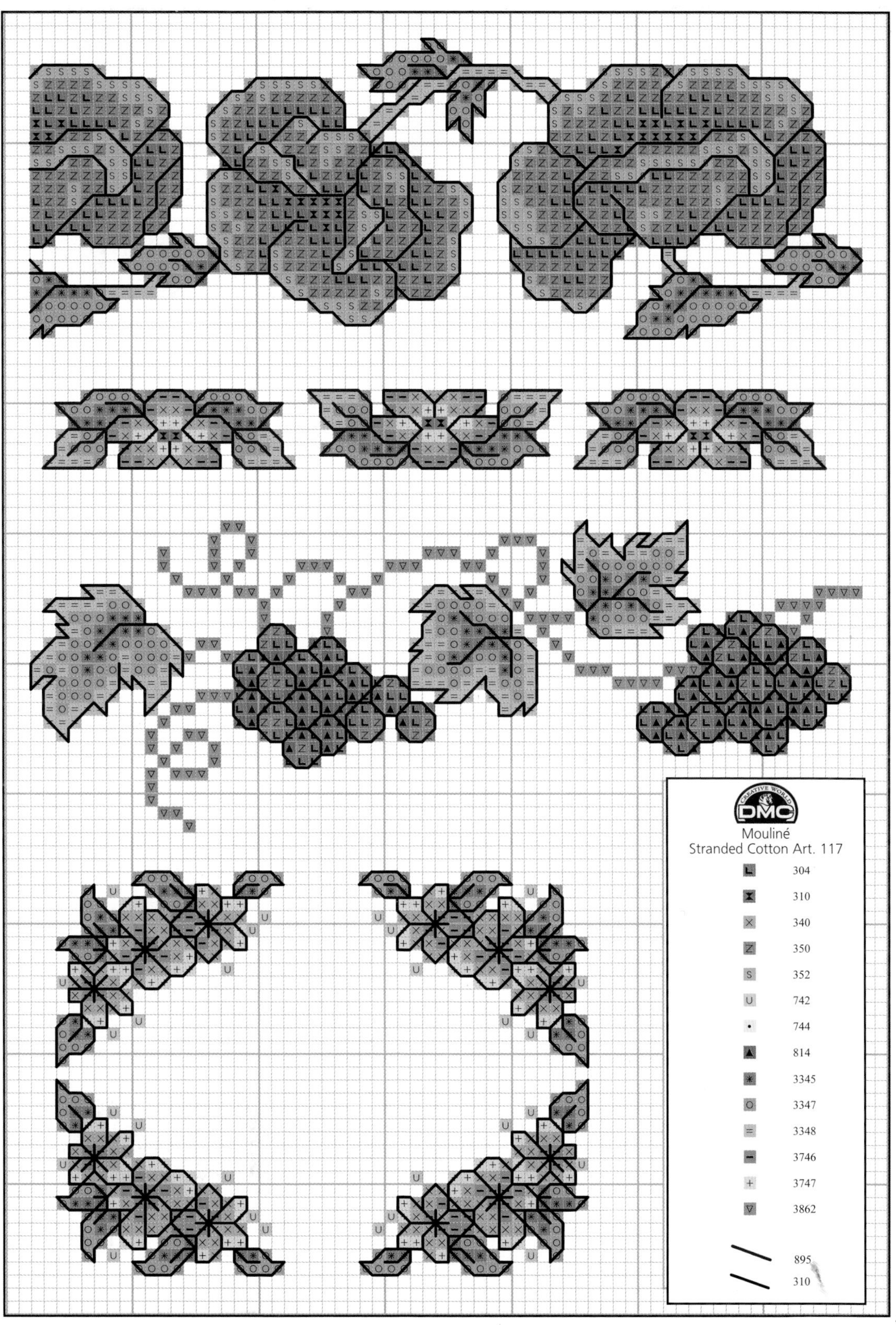
CREATIVE WORLD
DMC
Mouliné
Stranded Cotton Art. 117
304
310
340
350
352
742
744
814
3345
3347
3348
3746
3747
3862
895
310

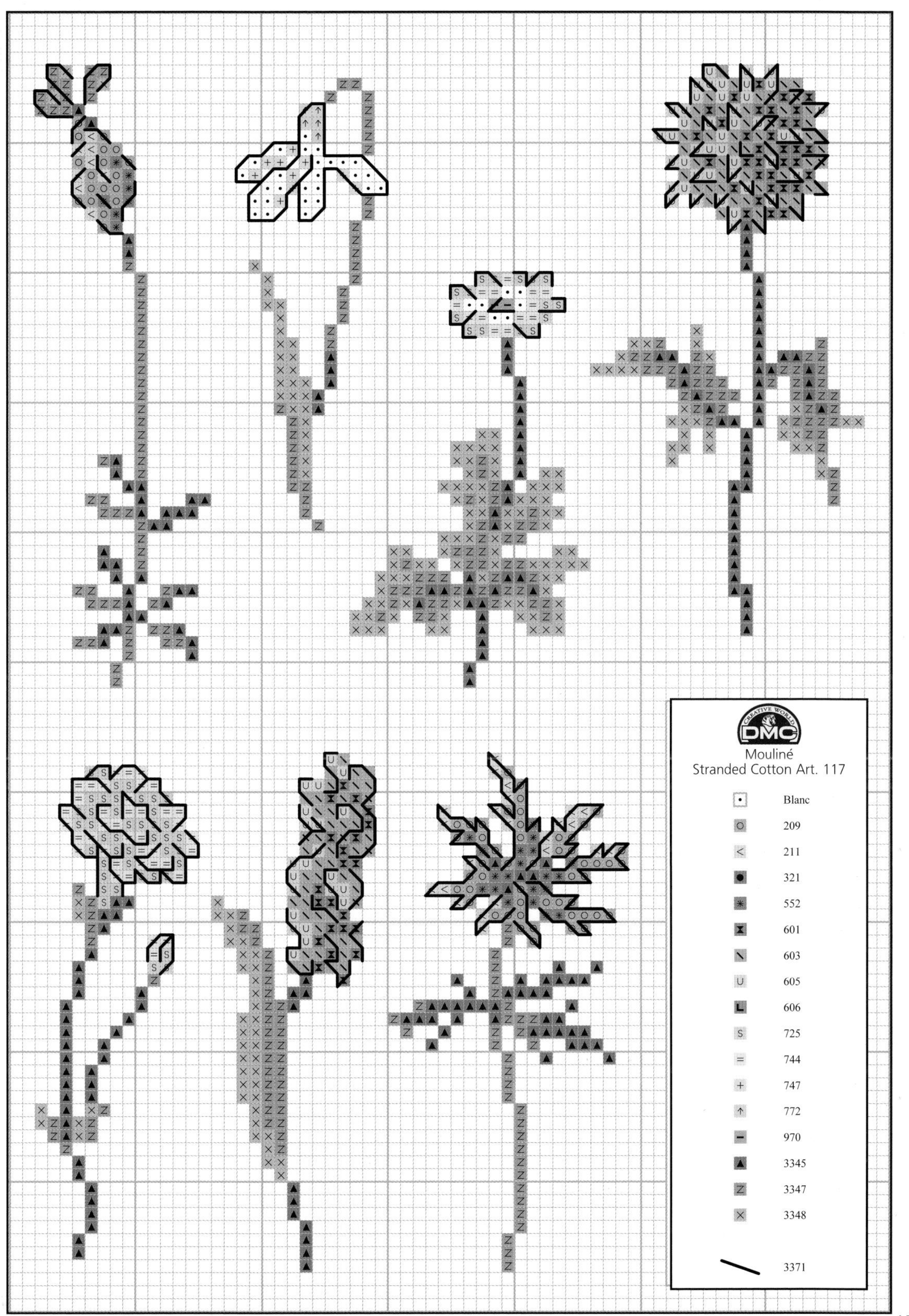
DMC
CREATIVE WORLD
Mouliné
Stranded Cotton Art. 117
Blanc
209
211
321
552
601
603
605
606
725
744
747
772
970
3345
3347
3348
3371

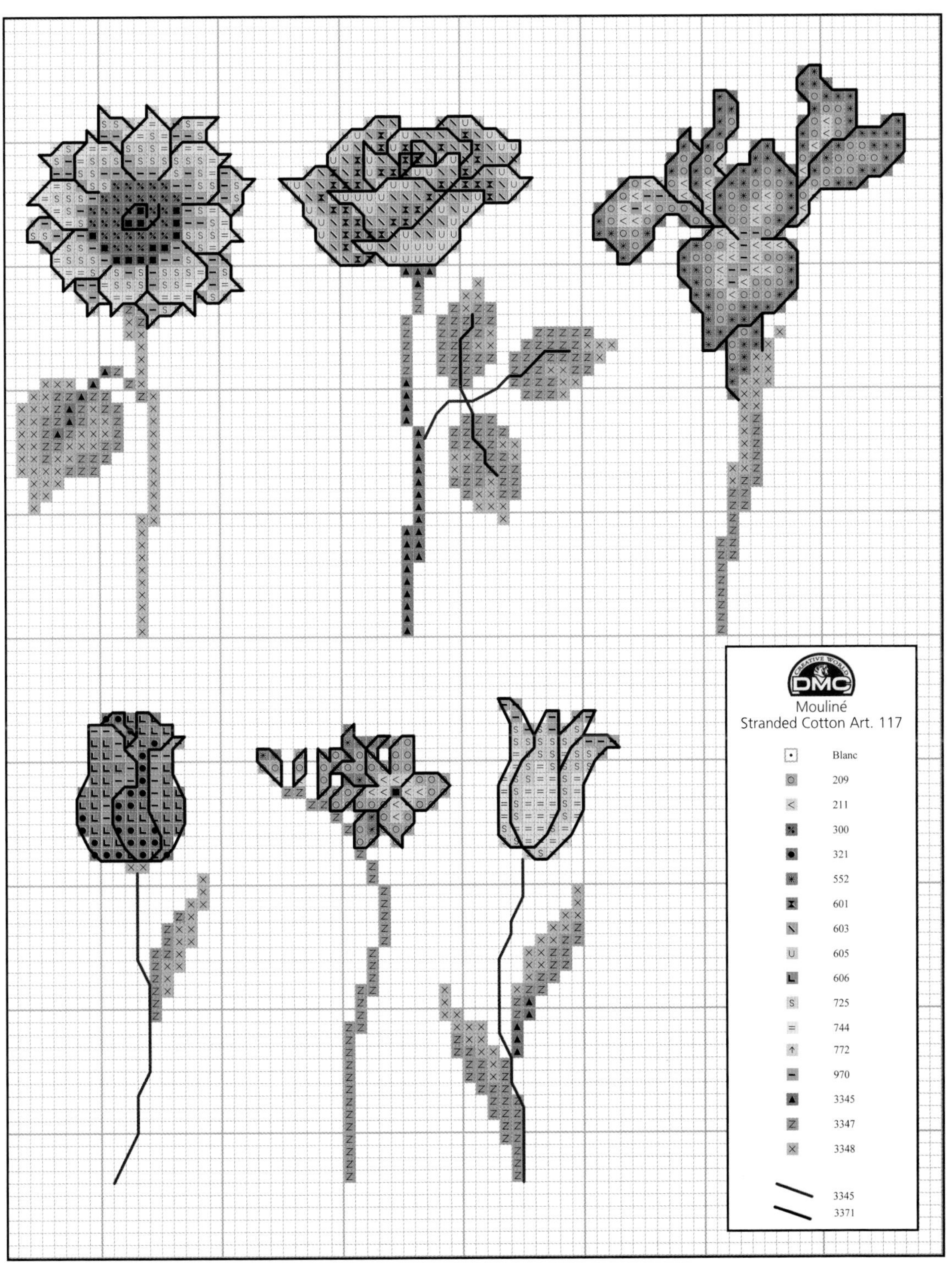
DMC
CREATIVE WORLD
Mouliné
Stranded Cotton Art. 117
Blanc
209
211
300
321
552
601
603
605
606
725
744
772
970
3345
3347
3348
3345
3371

43
44
45
46

47
48
49
50
51
52
53
54
55
56
57
58
59
60
61
62
63
64

DMC
CREATIVE WORLD
Mouliné
Stranded Cotton Art. 117
208
210
341
367
742
744
772
989
3021
3078
742
3021

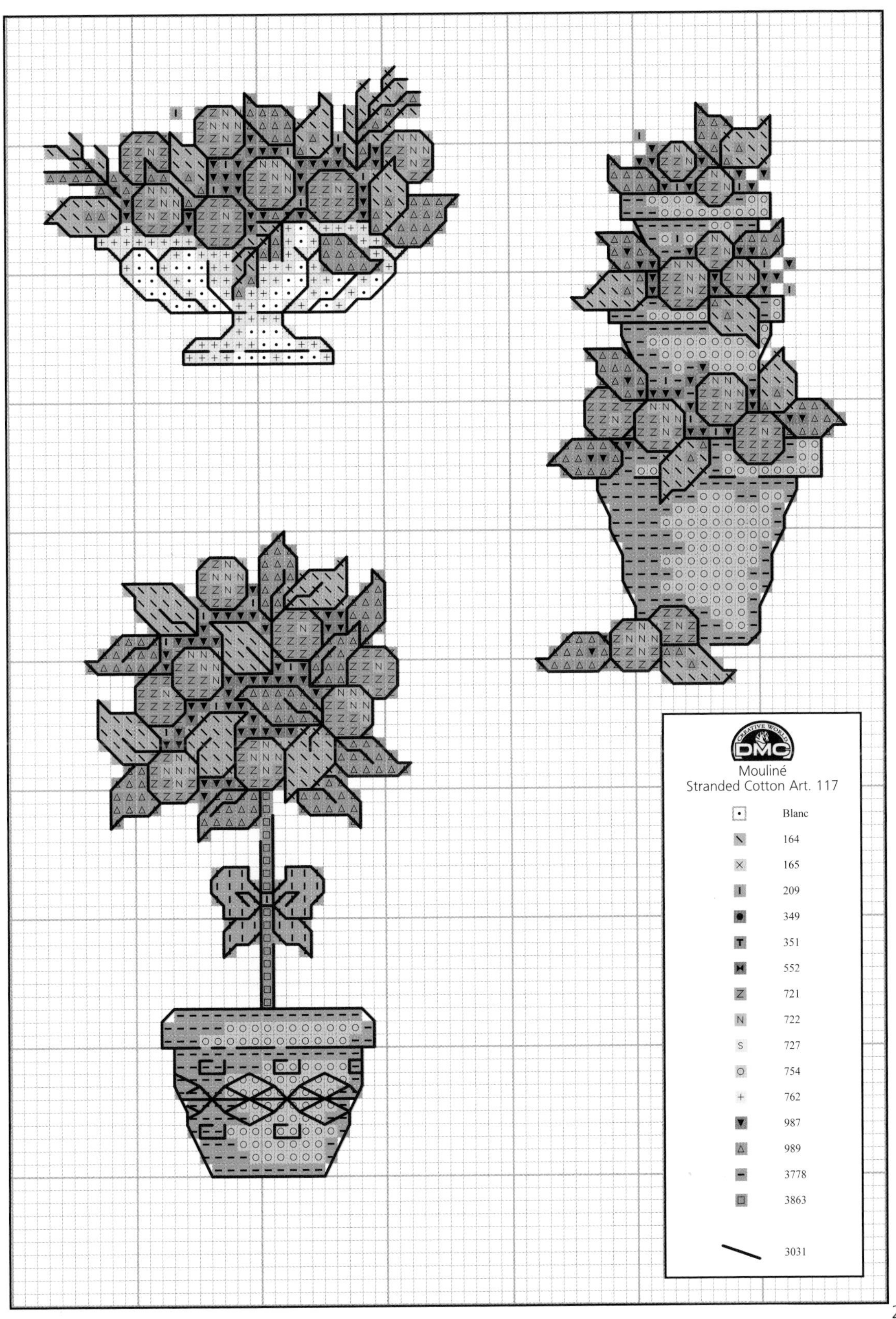
CREATIVE WORLD
DMC
Mouliné
Stranded Cotton Art. 117
Blanc
164
165
209
349
351
552
721
722
727
754
762
987
989
3778
3863
3031

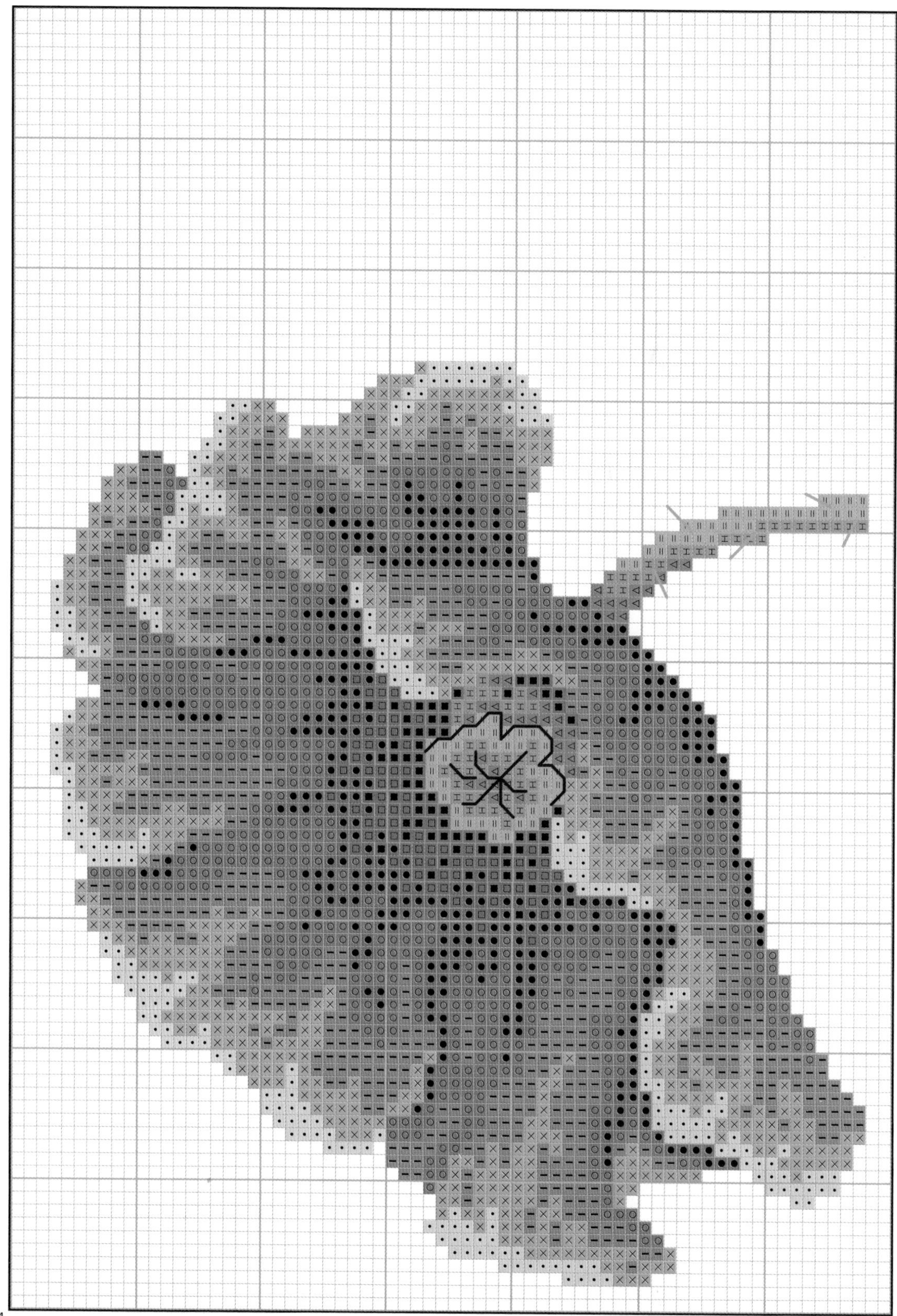

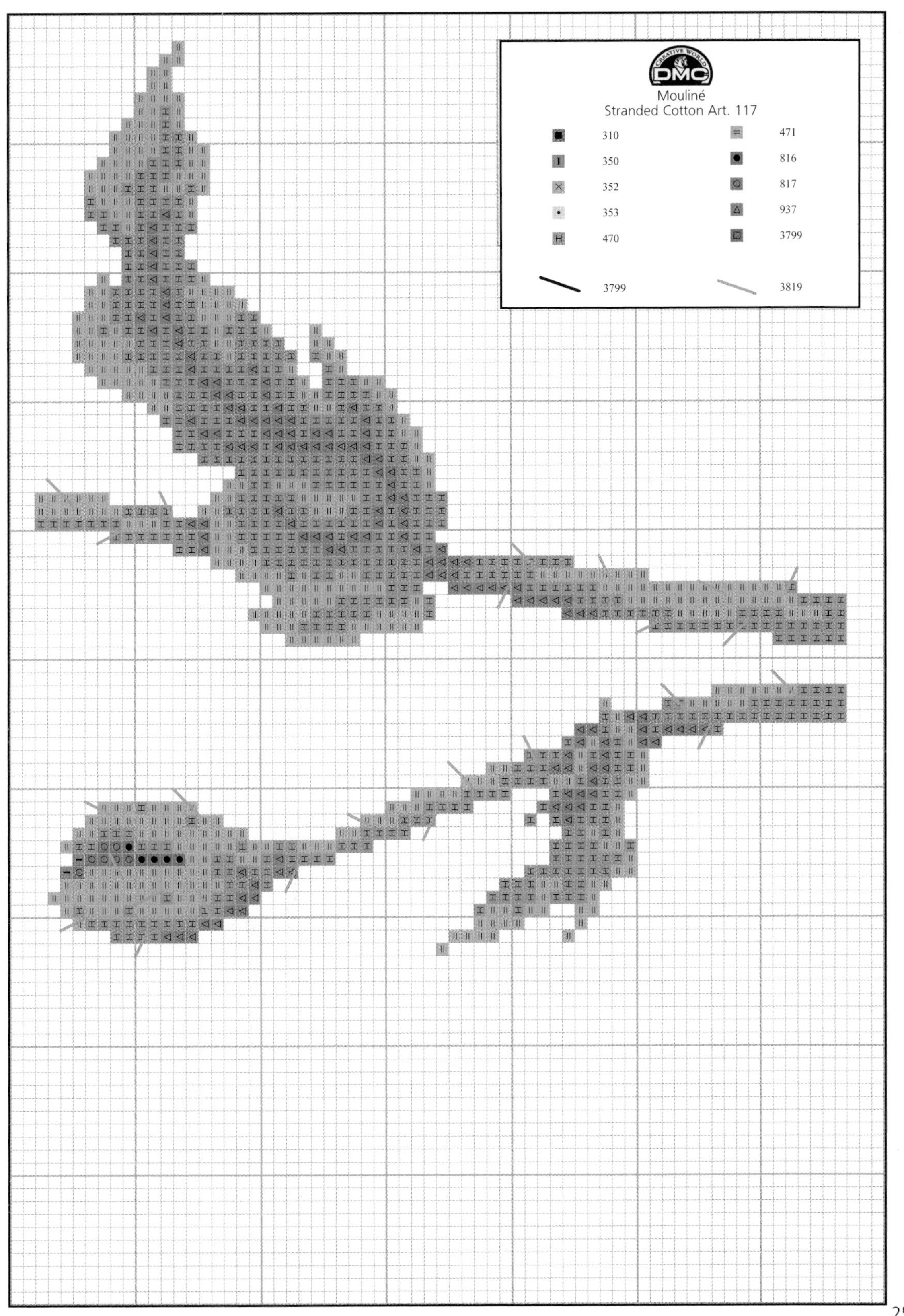
CREATIVE WORLD
DMC
Mouliné
Stranded Cotton Art. 117
310
350
352
353
470
471
816
817
937
3799
3799
3819

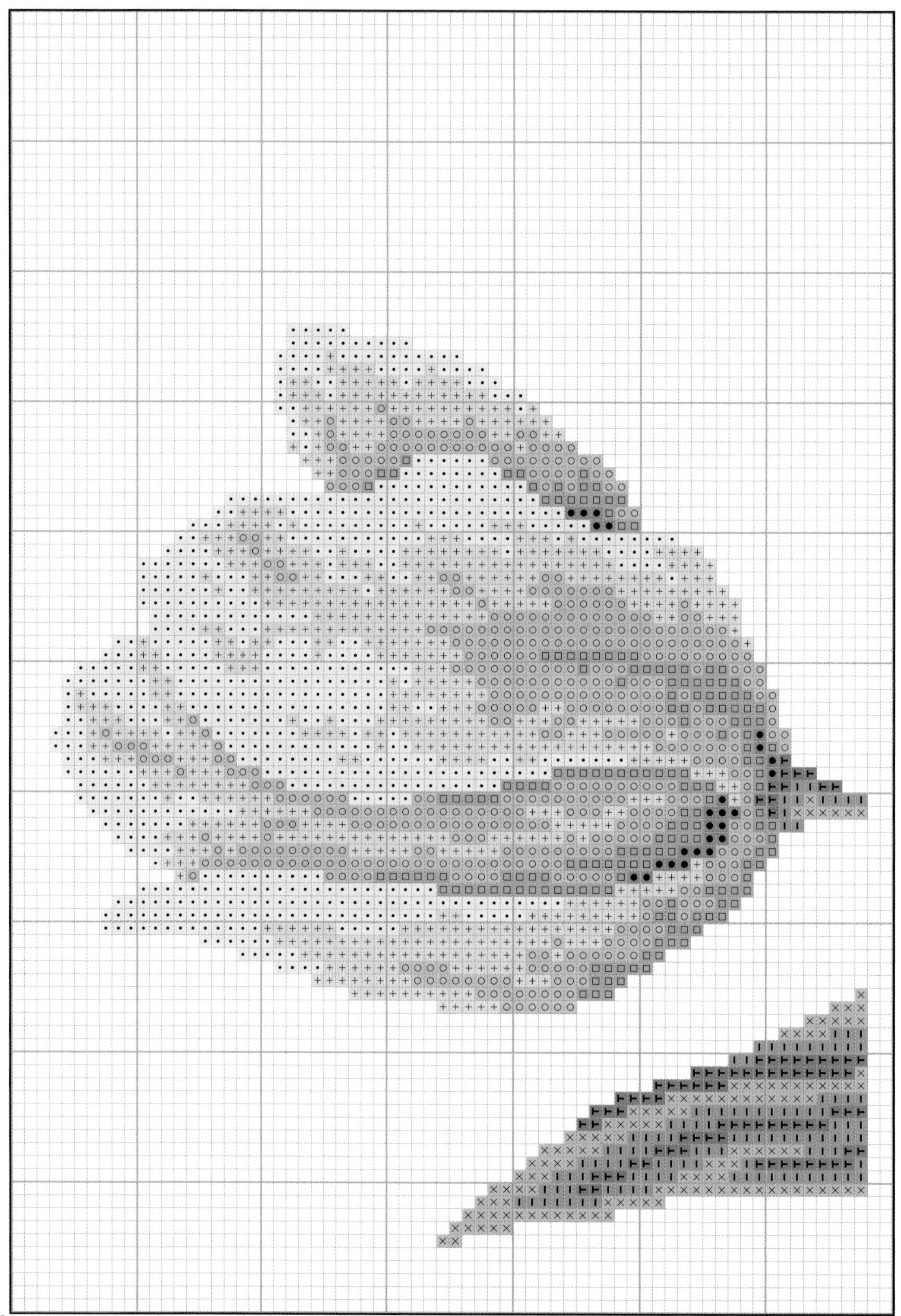

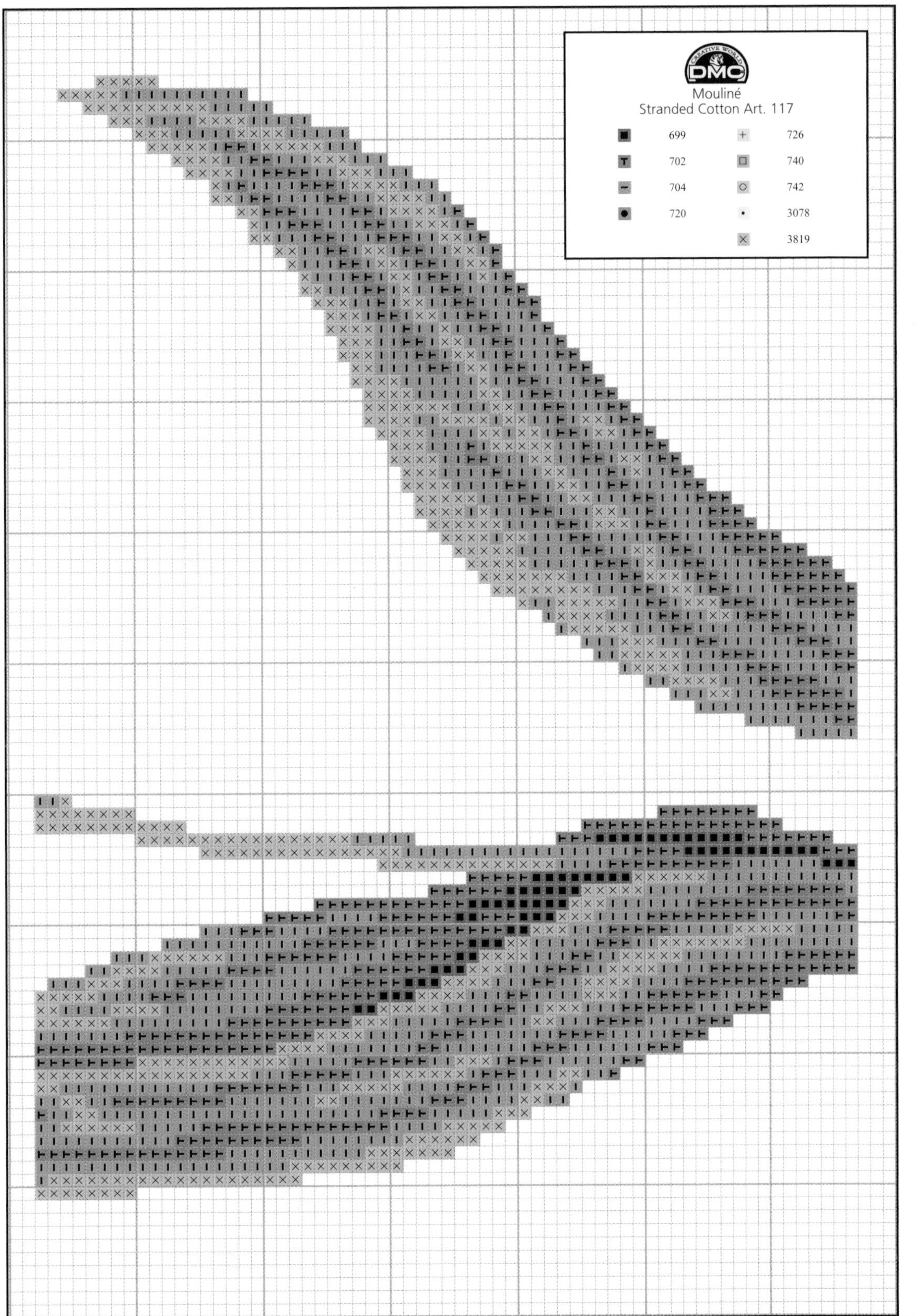
CREATIVE WORLD
DMC
Mouliné
Stranded Cotton Art. 117
699
702
704
720
726
740
742
3078
3819

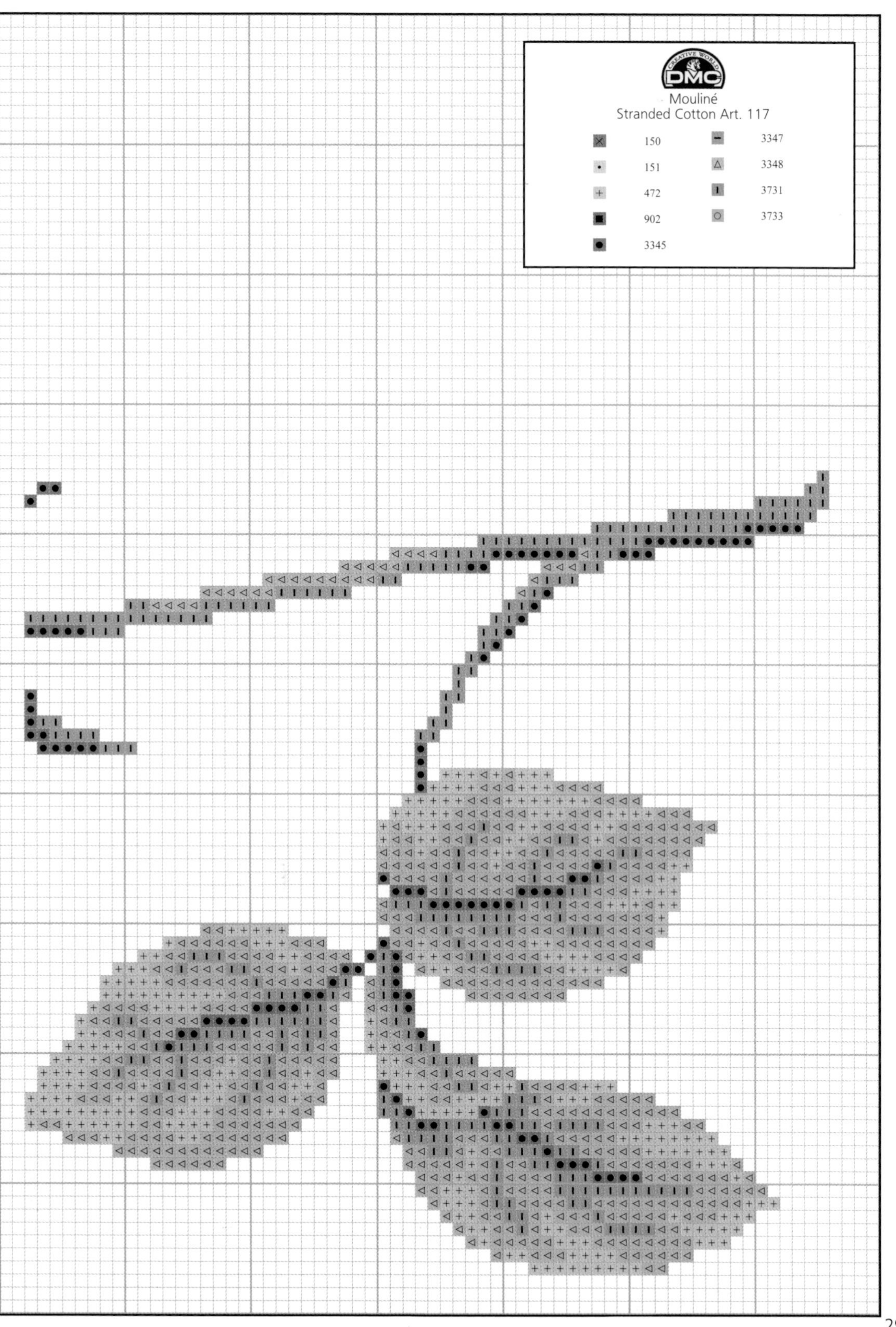
DMC
CREATIVE WORLD
Mouliné
Stranded Cotton Art. 117
150
151
472
902
3345
3347
3348
3731
3733

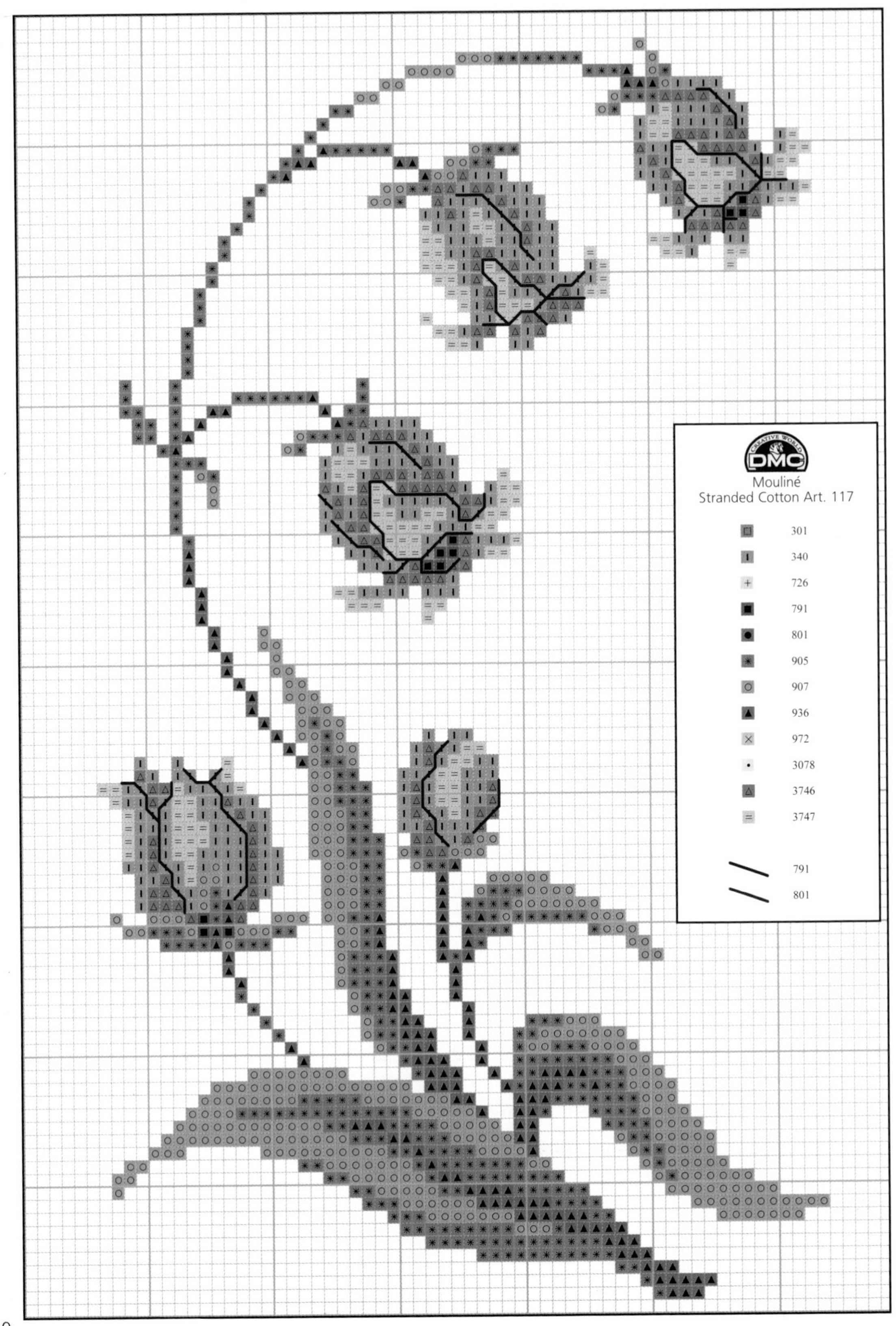
CREATIVE WORLD
DMC
Mouliné
Stranded Cotton Art. 117
301
340
726
791
801
905
907
936
972
3078
3746
3747
791
801

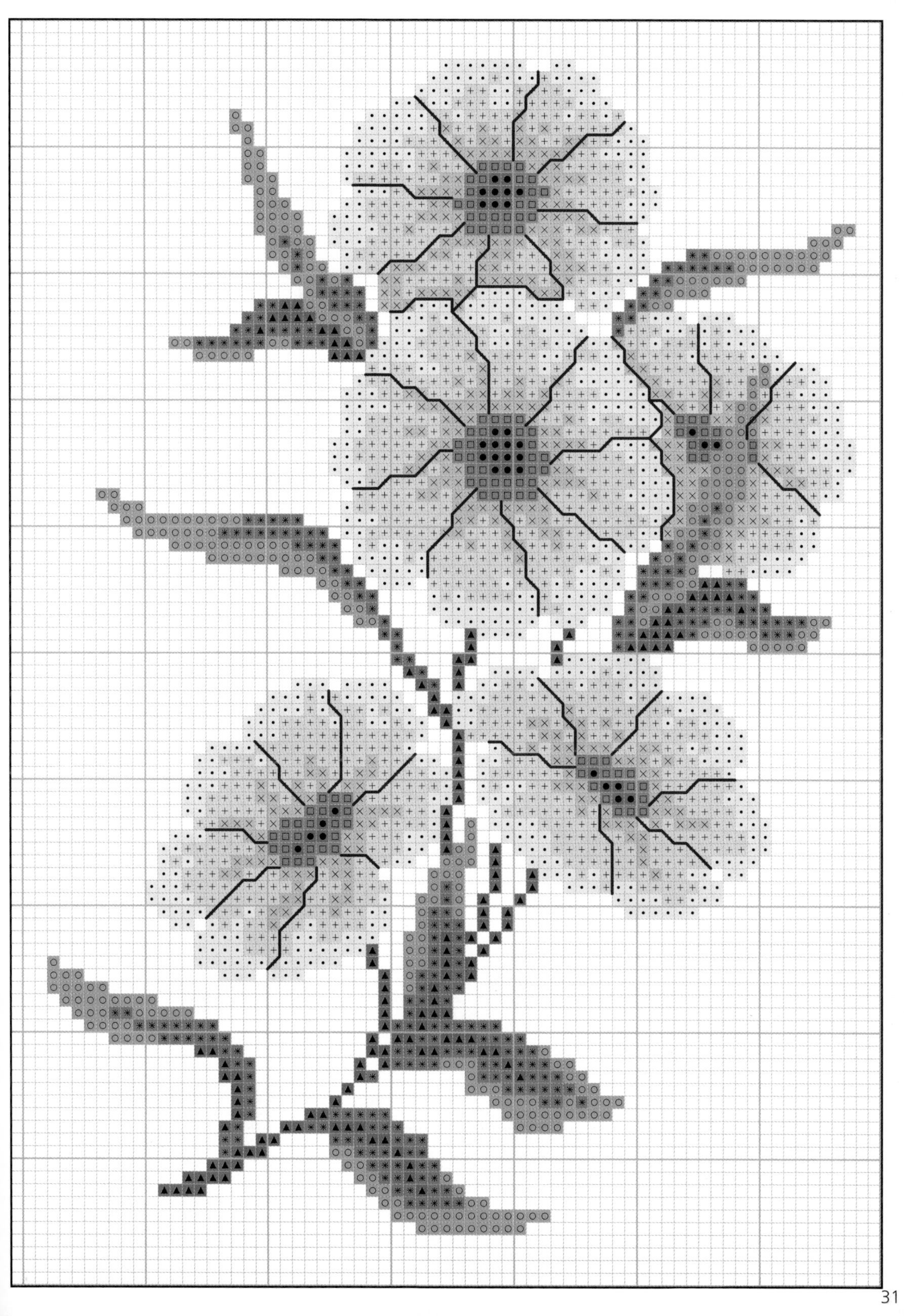

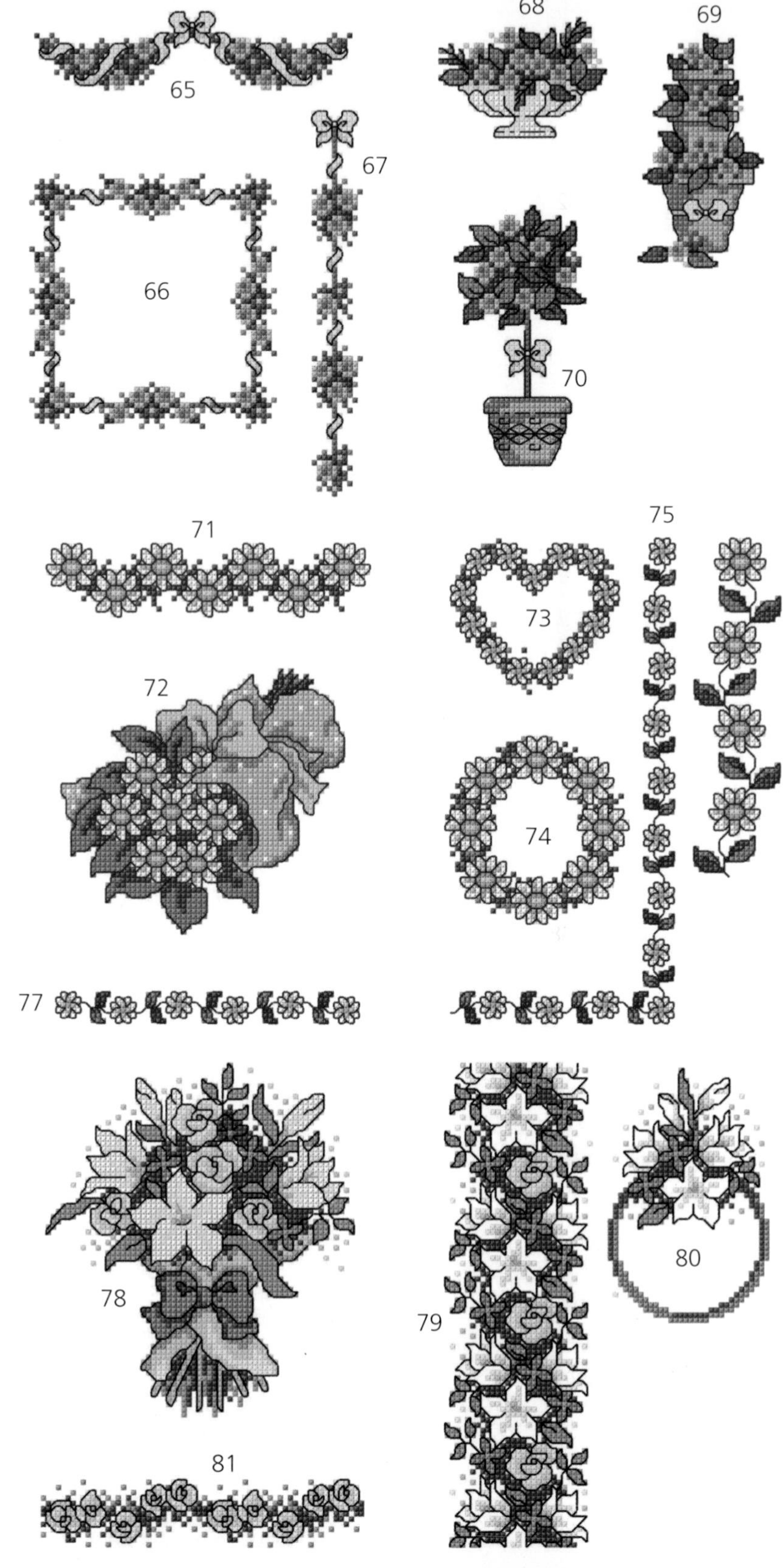
65
66
67
68
69
70
71
72
73
74
75
77
78
79
80
81

82
83
84
86
87
85
89
88
91
92
90
93

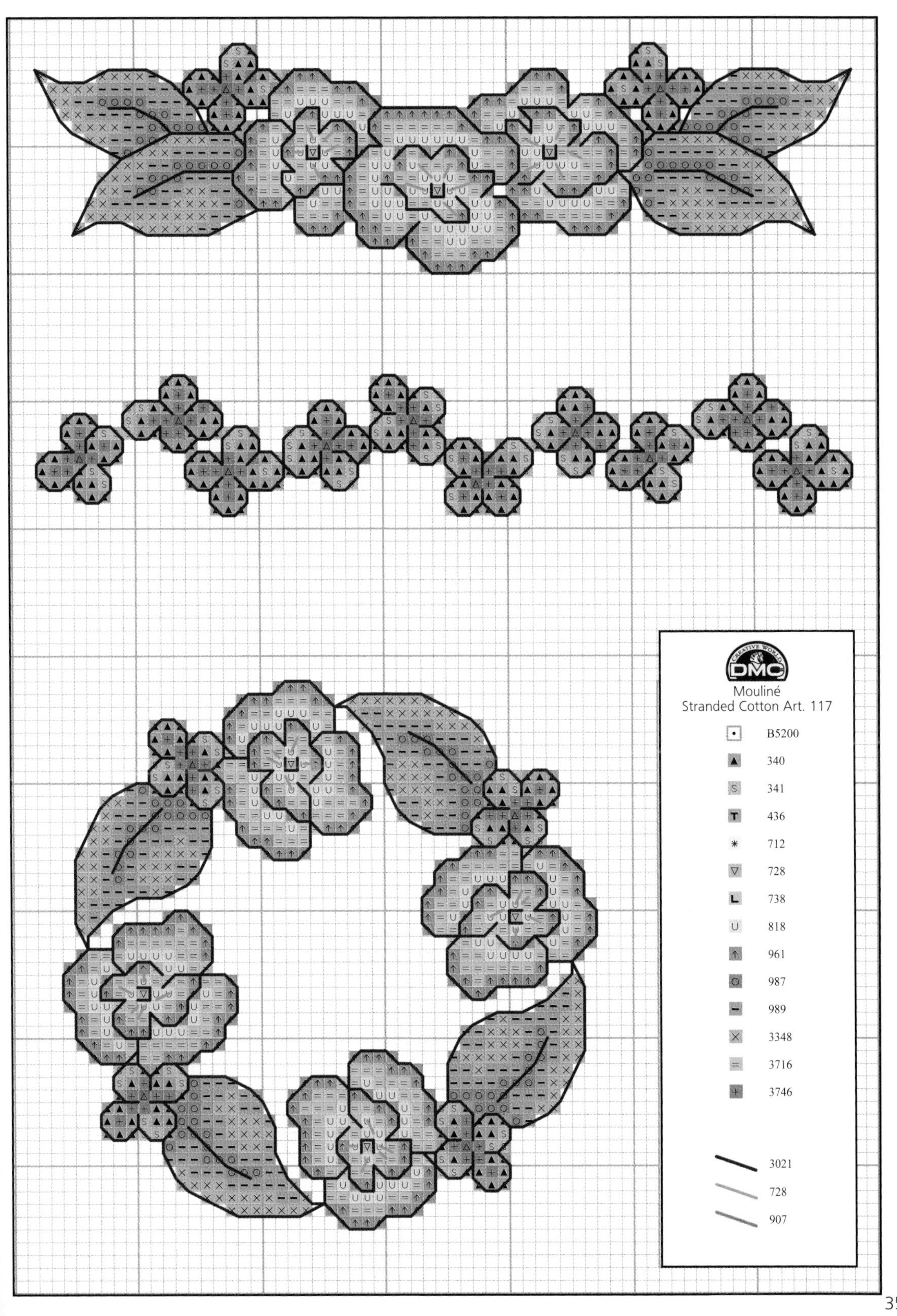
DMC
CREATIVE WORLD
Mouliné
Stranded Cotton Art. 117
B5200
340
341
436
712
728
738
818
961
987
989
3348
3716
3746
3021
728
907

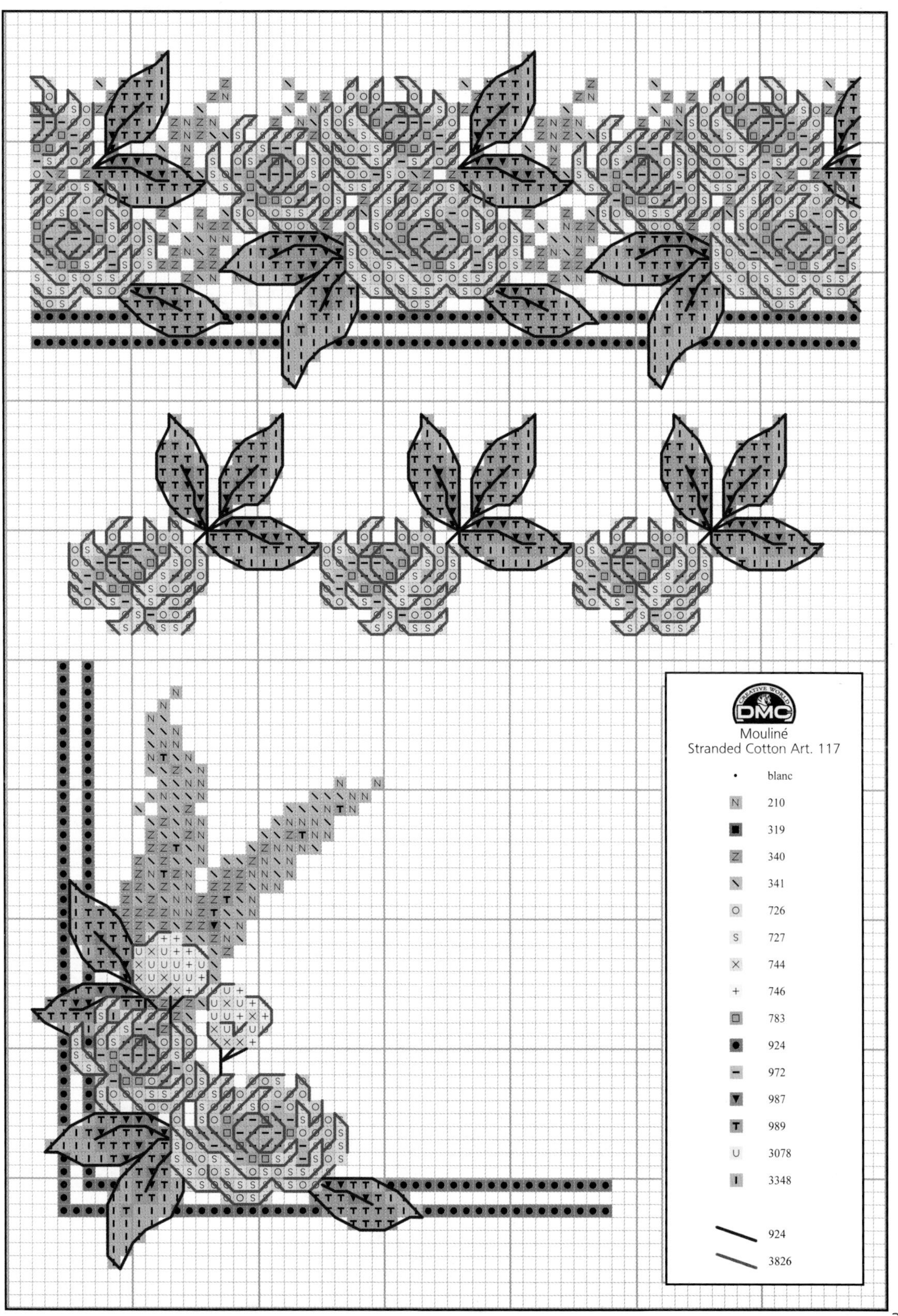
DMC
CREATIVE WORLD
Mouliné
Stranded Cotton Art. 117
• blanc
N 210
■ 319
Z 340
\ 341
O 726
S 727
× 744
+ 746
□ 783
● 924
− 972
▼ 987
T 989
U 3078
I 3348
924
3826

DMC
CREATIVE WORLD
Mouliné
Stranded Cotton Art. 117
150
340
445
818
957
987
3348
3731
3733
3031

DMC
CREATIVE WORLD
Mouliné
Stranded Cotton Art. 117
Blanc
164
208
210
742
744
746
772
987
742
3031

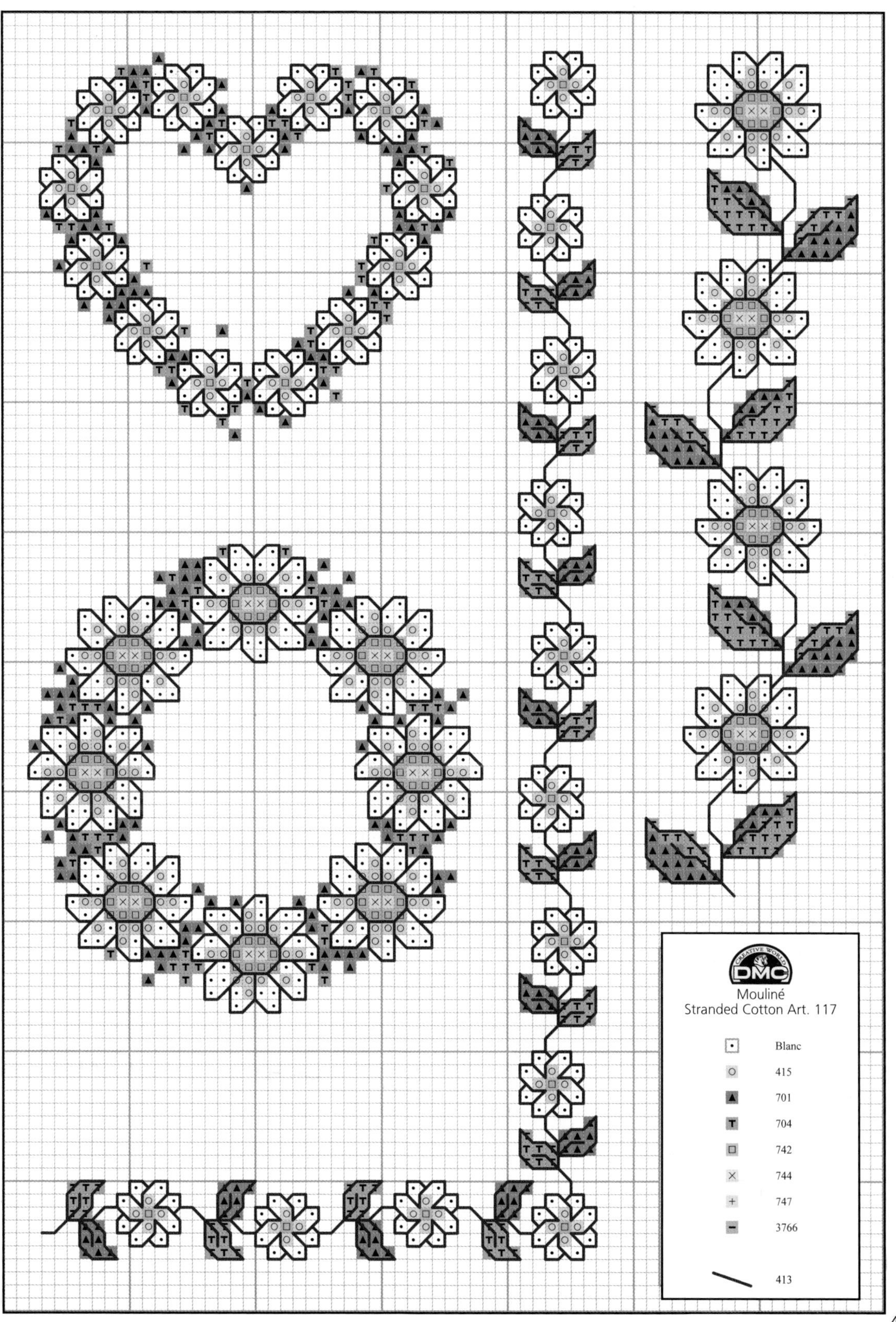
DMC CREATIVE WORLD
Mouliné
Stranded Cotton Art. 117
Blanc
415
701
704
742
744
747
3766
413

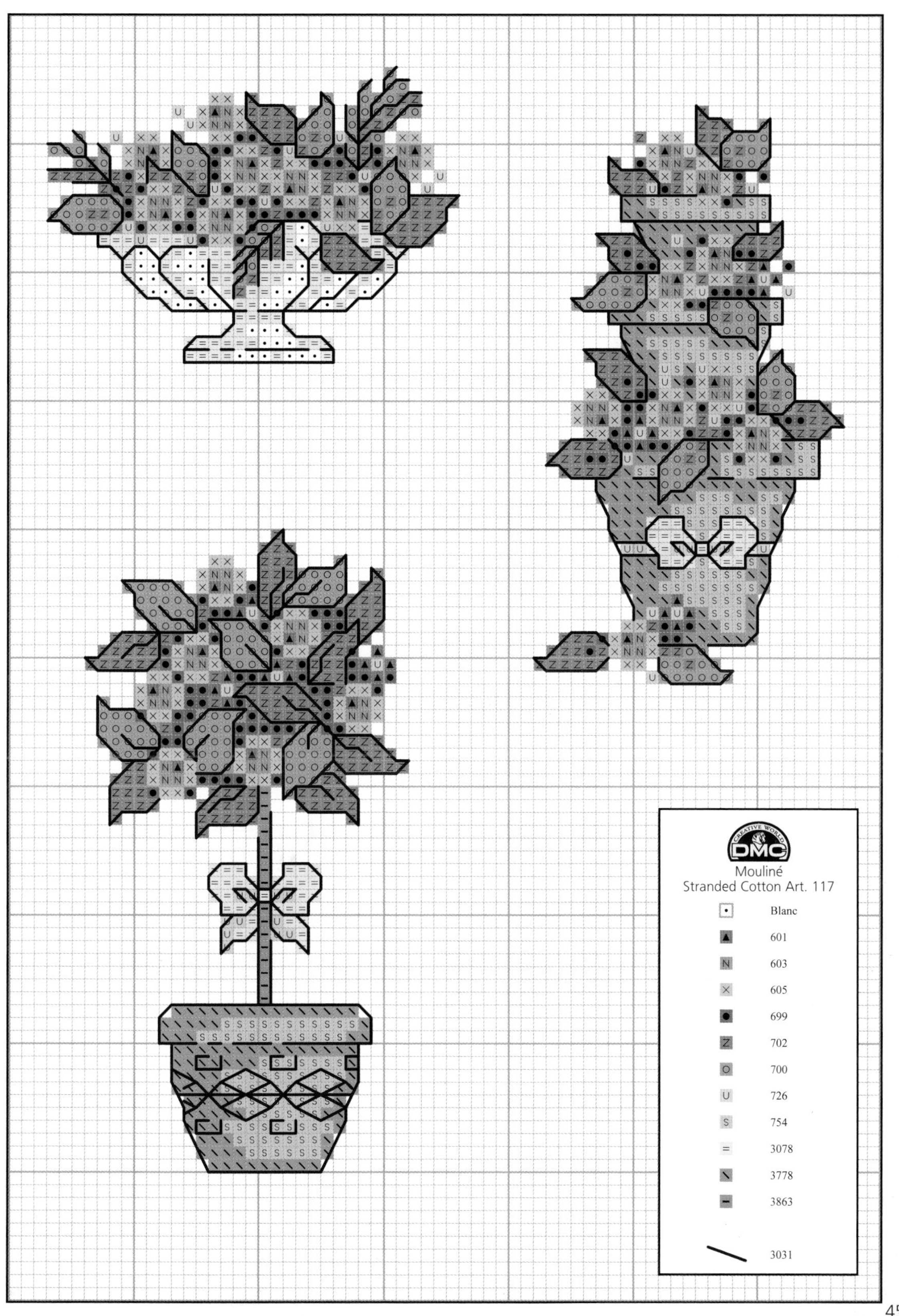
CREATIVE WORLD
DMC
Mouliné
Stranded Cotton Art. 117
Blanc
601
603
605
699
702
700
726
754
3078
3778
3863
3031

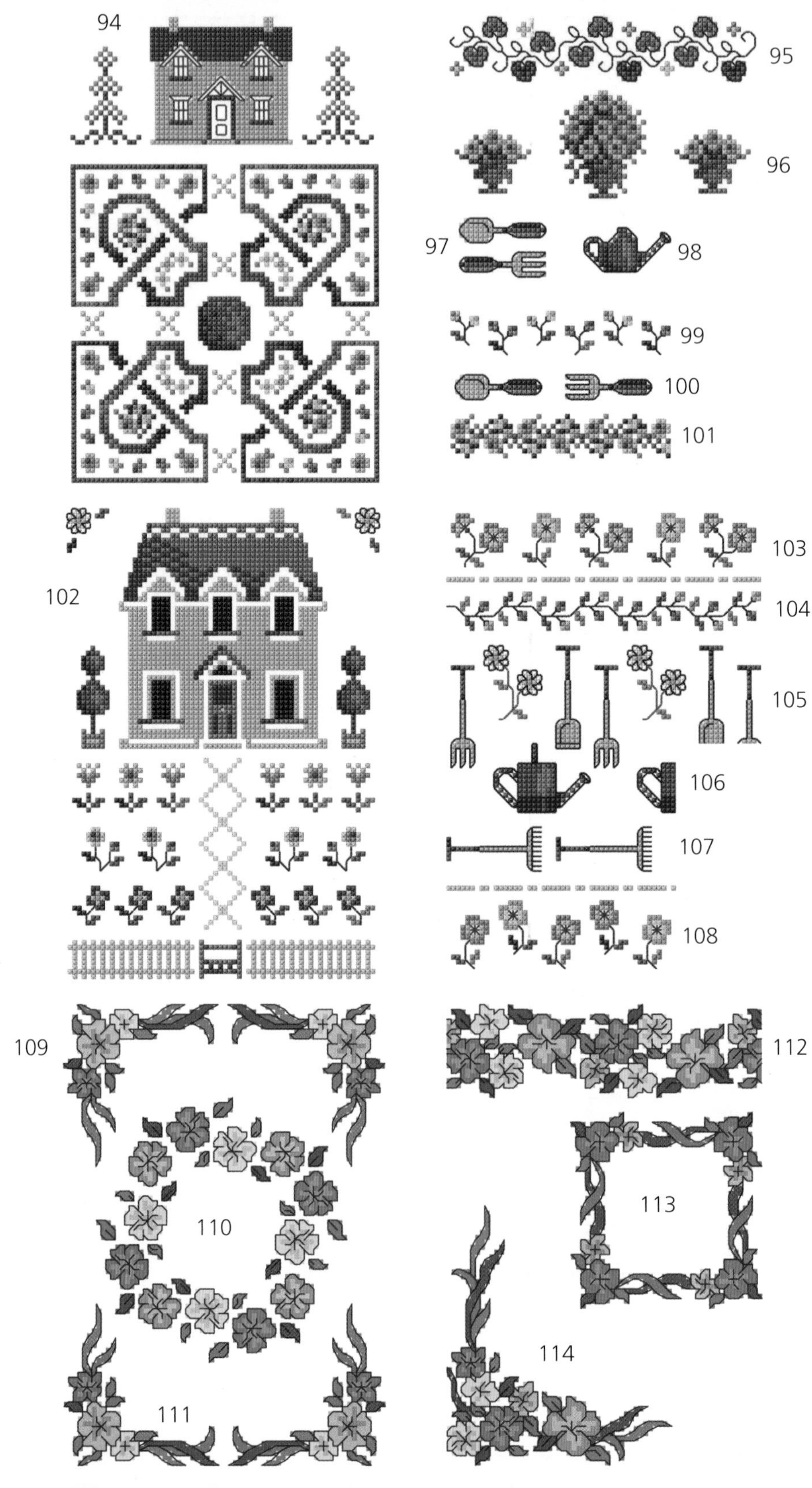
94
95
96
97
98
99
100
101
102
103
104
105
106
107
108
109
110
111
112
113
114

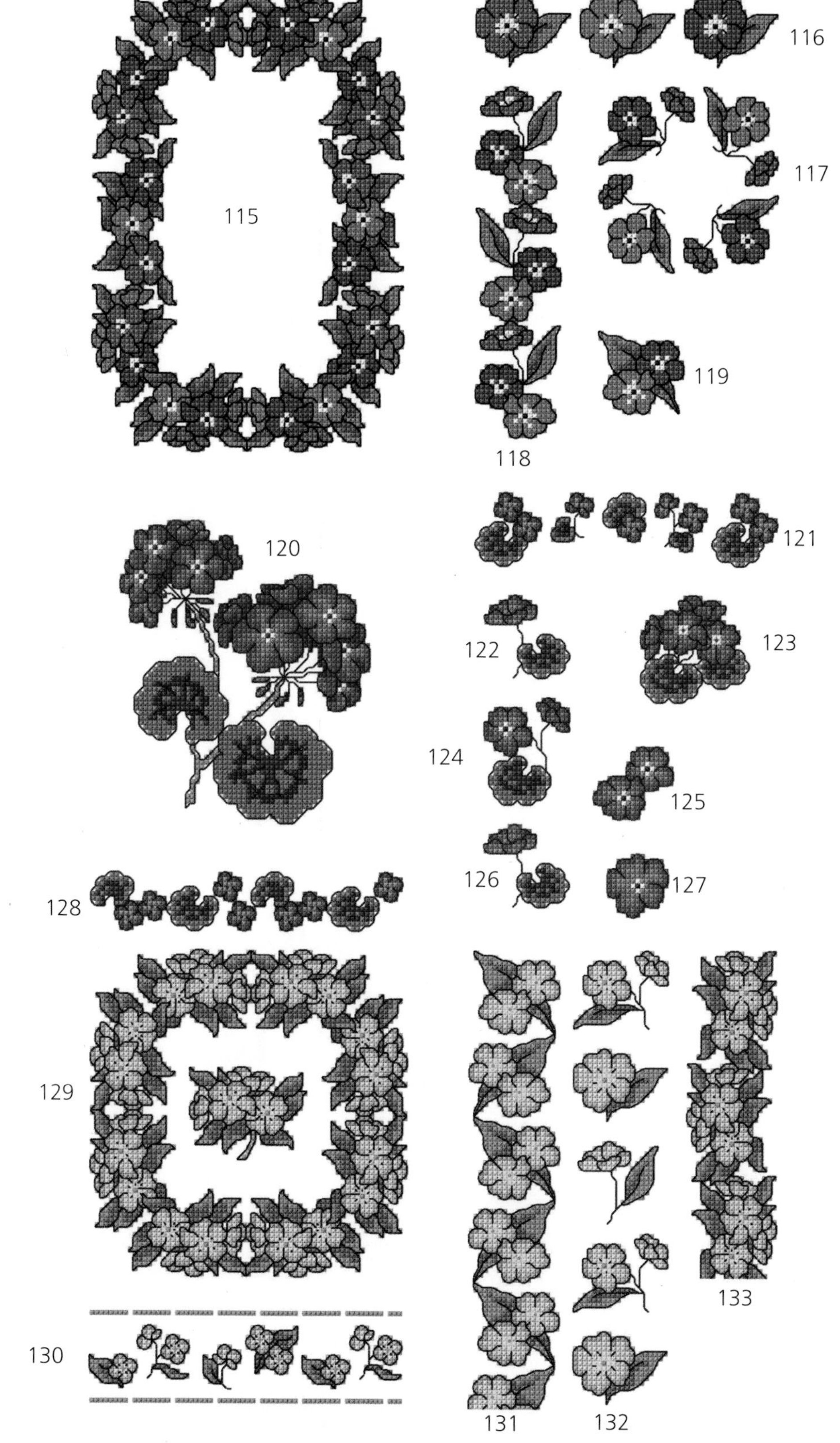
115
116
117
118
119
120
121
122
123
124
125
126
127
128
129
130
131
132
133

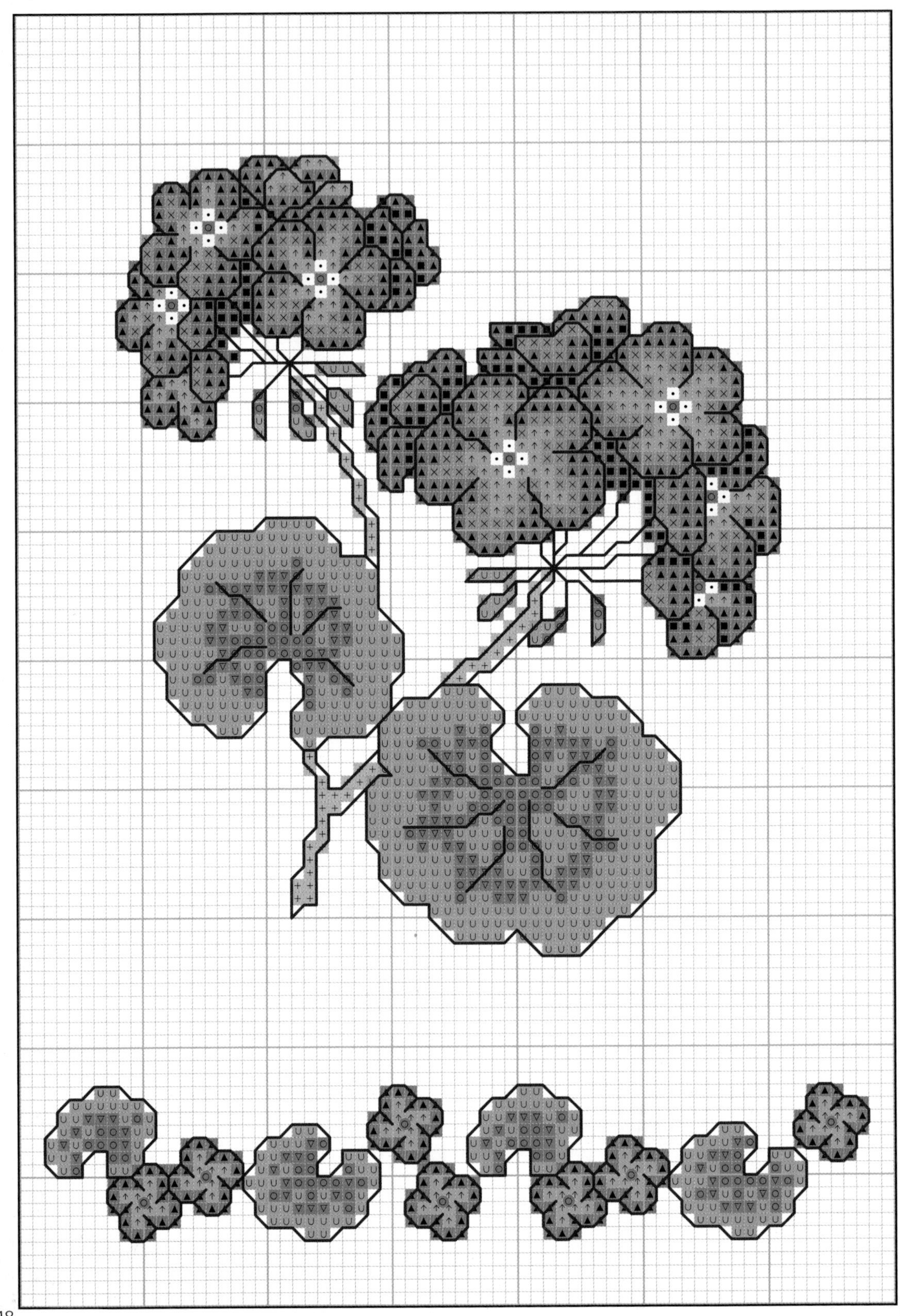

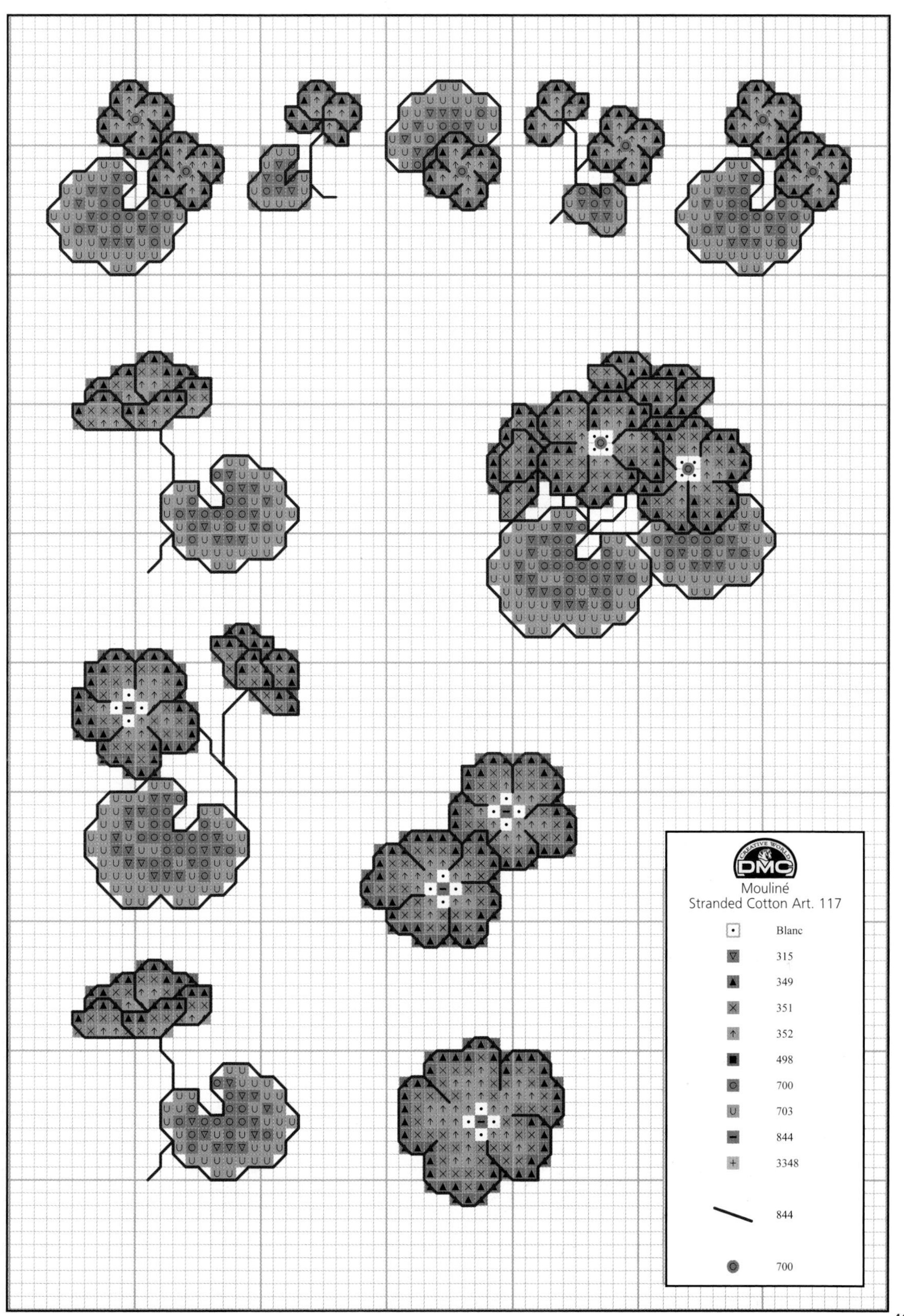
DMC
CREATIVE WORLD
Mouliné
Stranded Cotton Art. 117
Blanc
315
349
351
352
498
700
703
844
3348
844
700

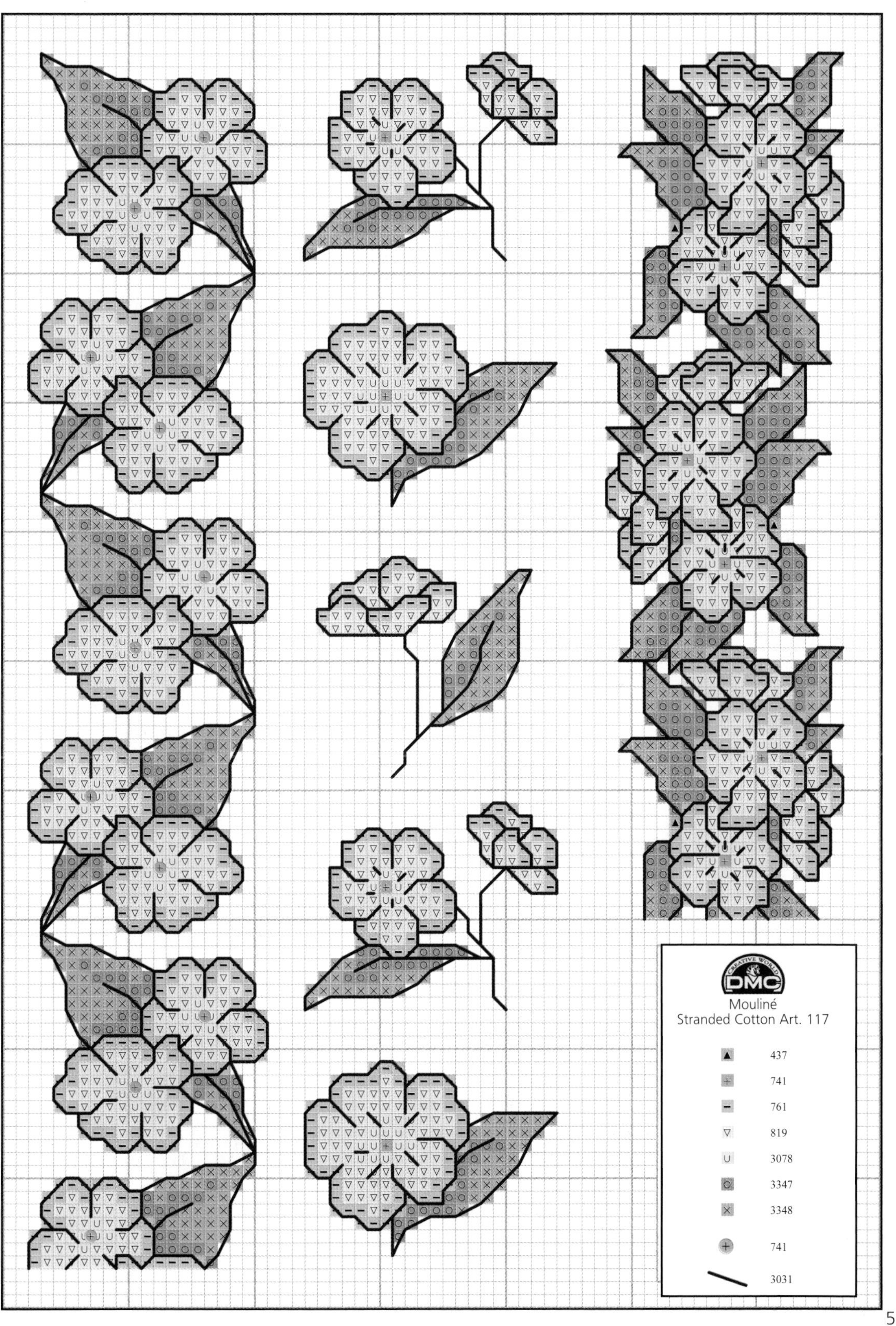
DMC
CREATIVE WORLD
Mouliné
Stranded Cotton Art. 117
437
741
761
819
3078
3347
3348
741
3031

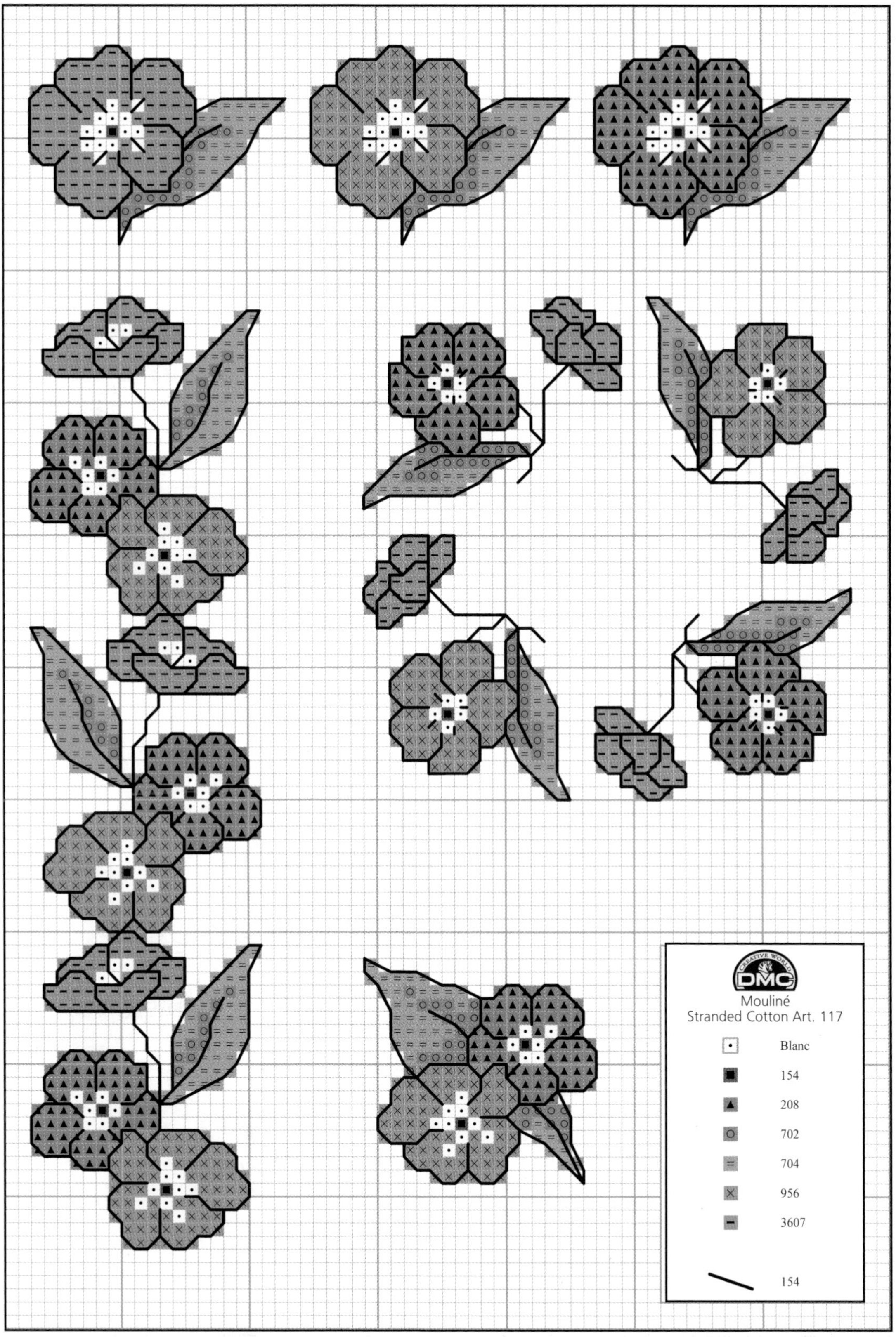
DMC
CREATIVE WORLD
Mouliné
Stranded Cotton Art. 117
Blanc
154
208
702
704
956
3607
154

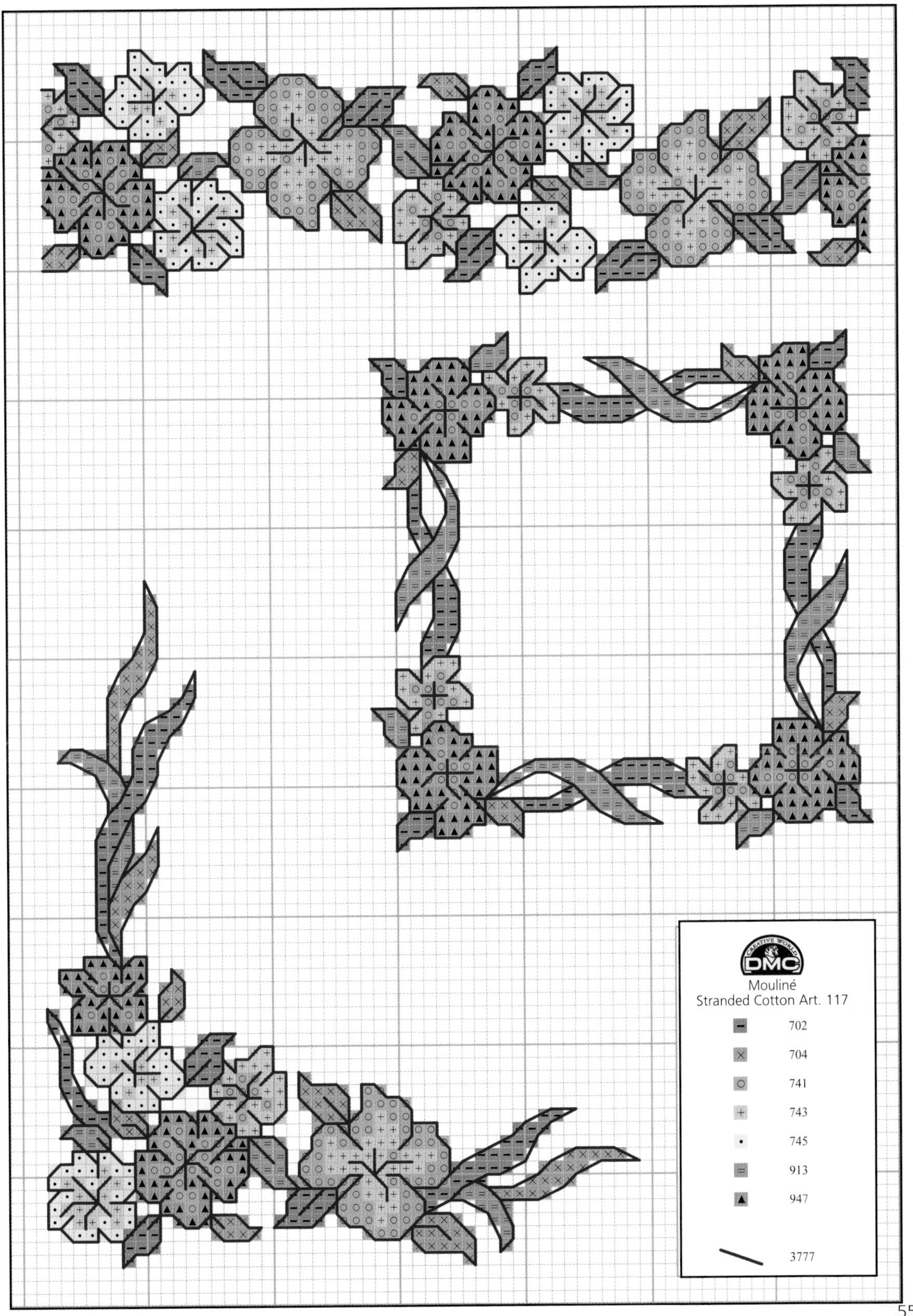
DMC
CREATIVE WORLD
Mouliné
Stranded Cotton Art. 117
702
704
741
743
745
913
947
3777

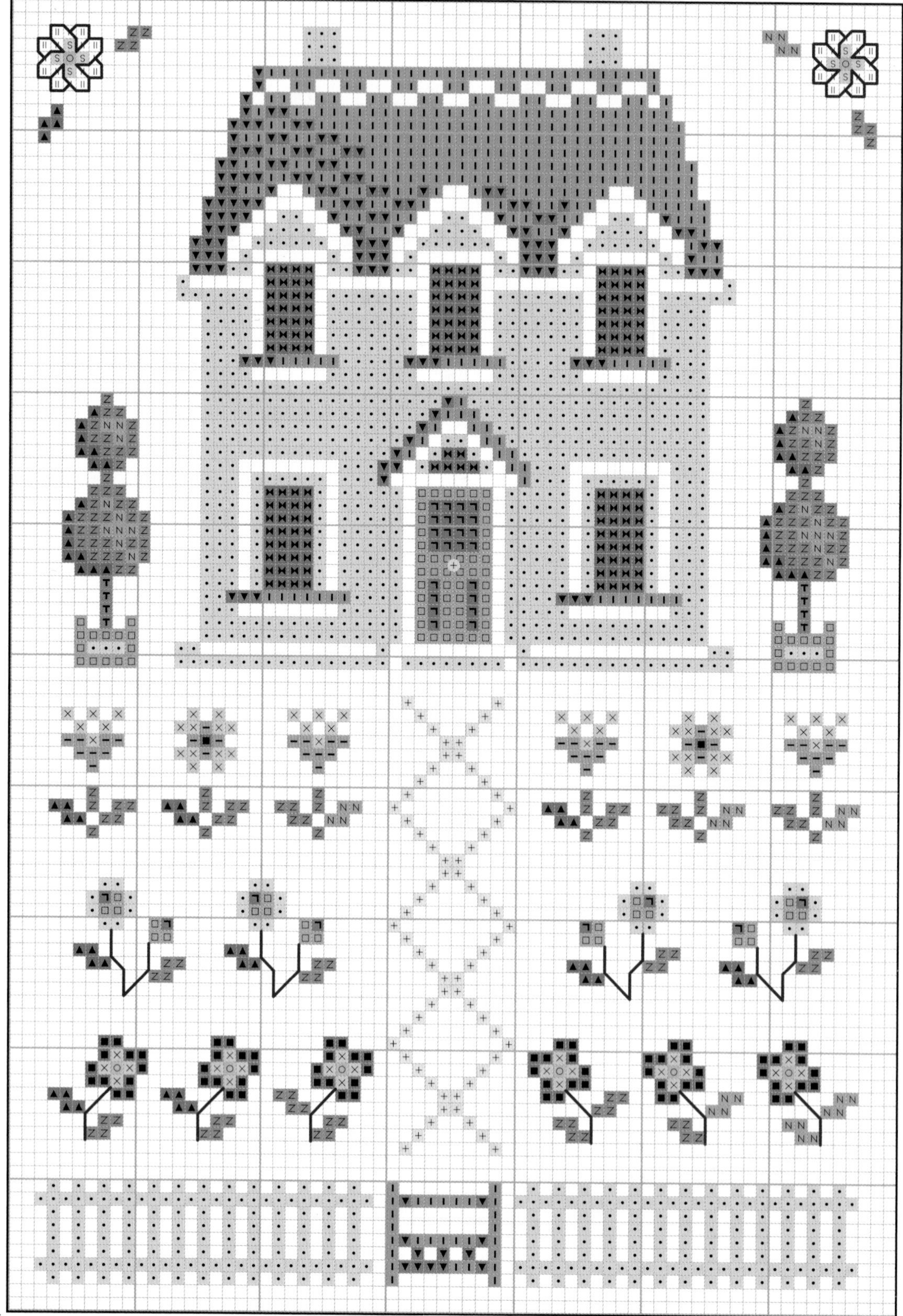

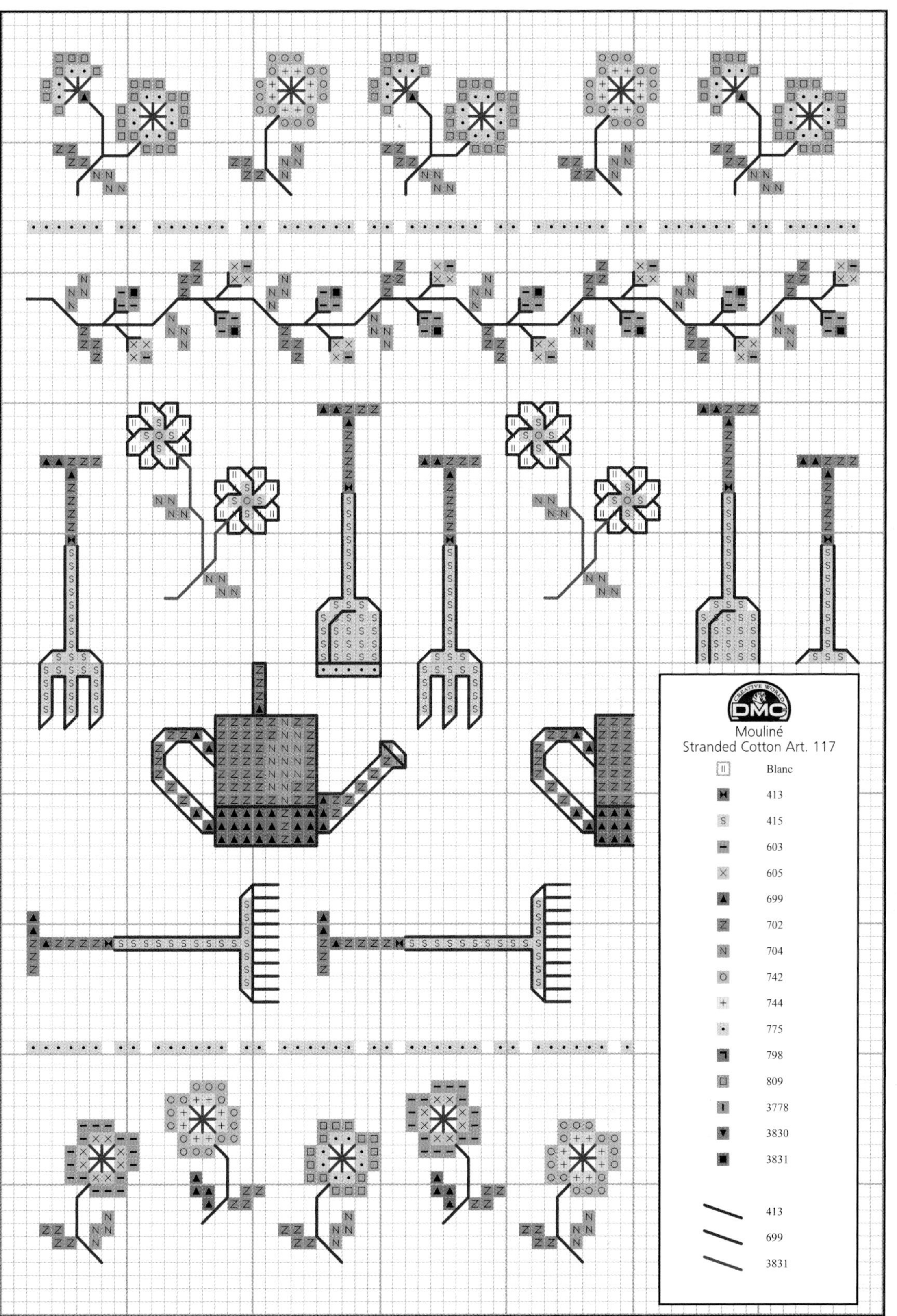

CREATIVE WORLD
DMC
Mouliné
Stranded Cotton Art. 117
Blanc
413
415
603
605
699
702
704
742
744
775
798
809
3778
3830
3831
413
699
3831

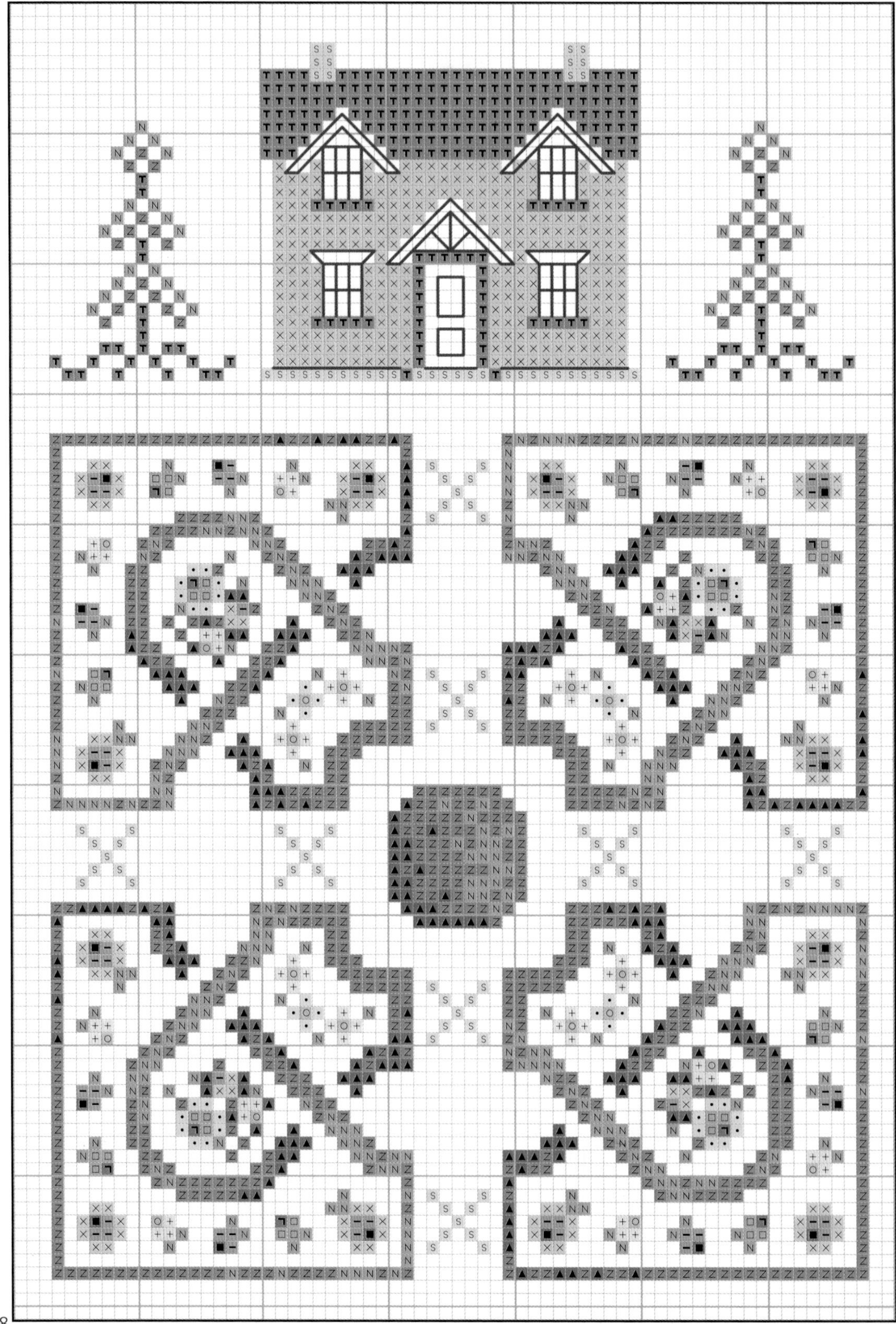

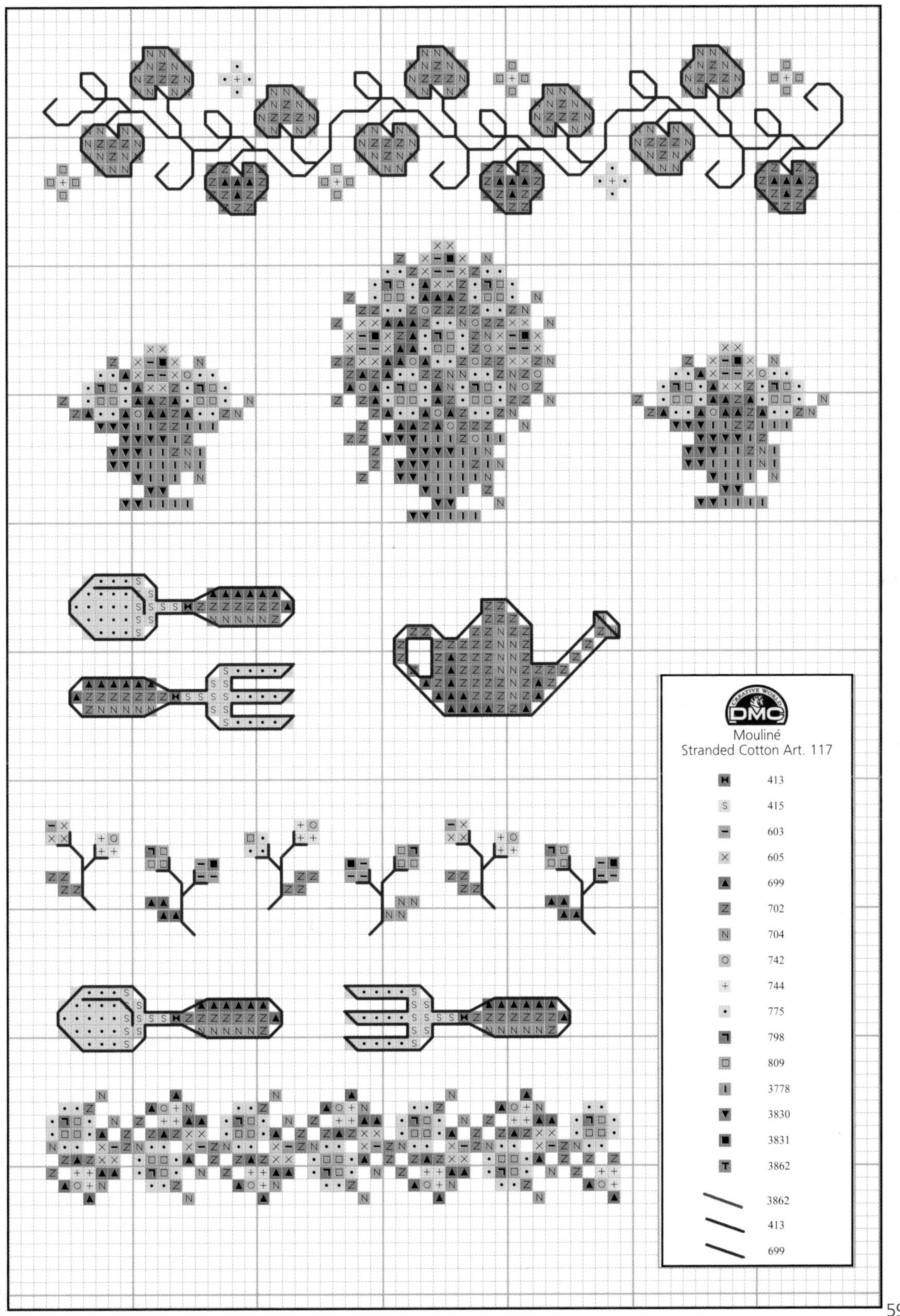
DMC
Mouliné
Stranded Cotton Art. 117
413
415
603
605
699
702
704
742
744
775
798
809
3778
3830
3831
3862
3862
413
699

134 135

136

137

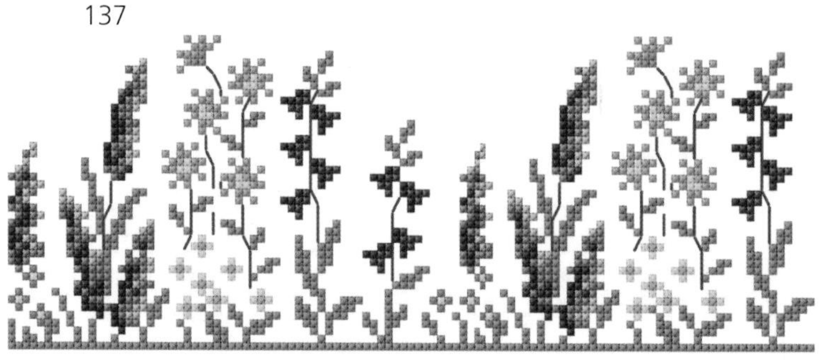

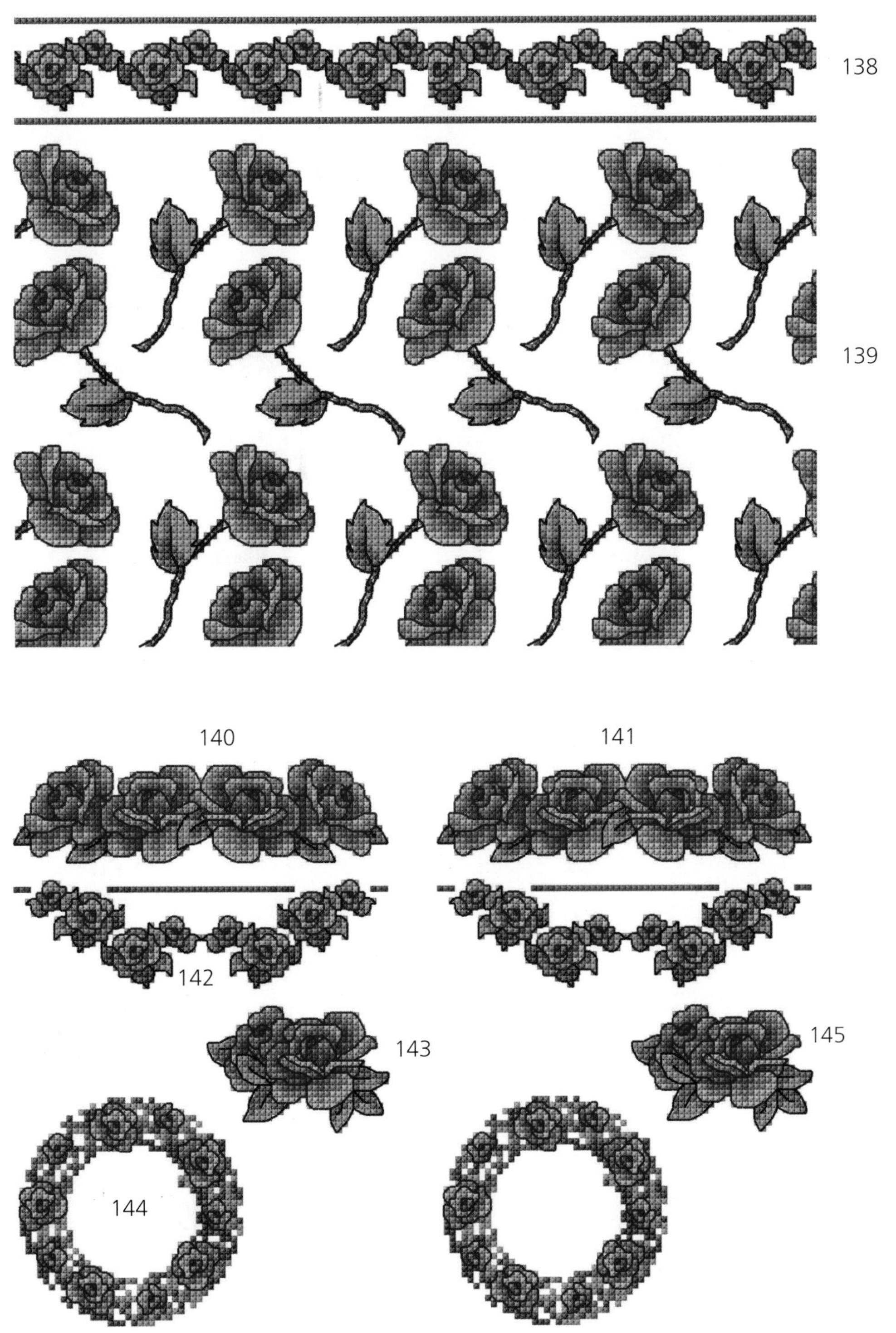
138
139
140
141
142
143
145
144

CREATIVE WORLD
DMC
Mouliné
Stranded Cotton Art. 117
150
151
895
3346
3347
3348
3685
3731
3733
3685

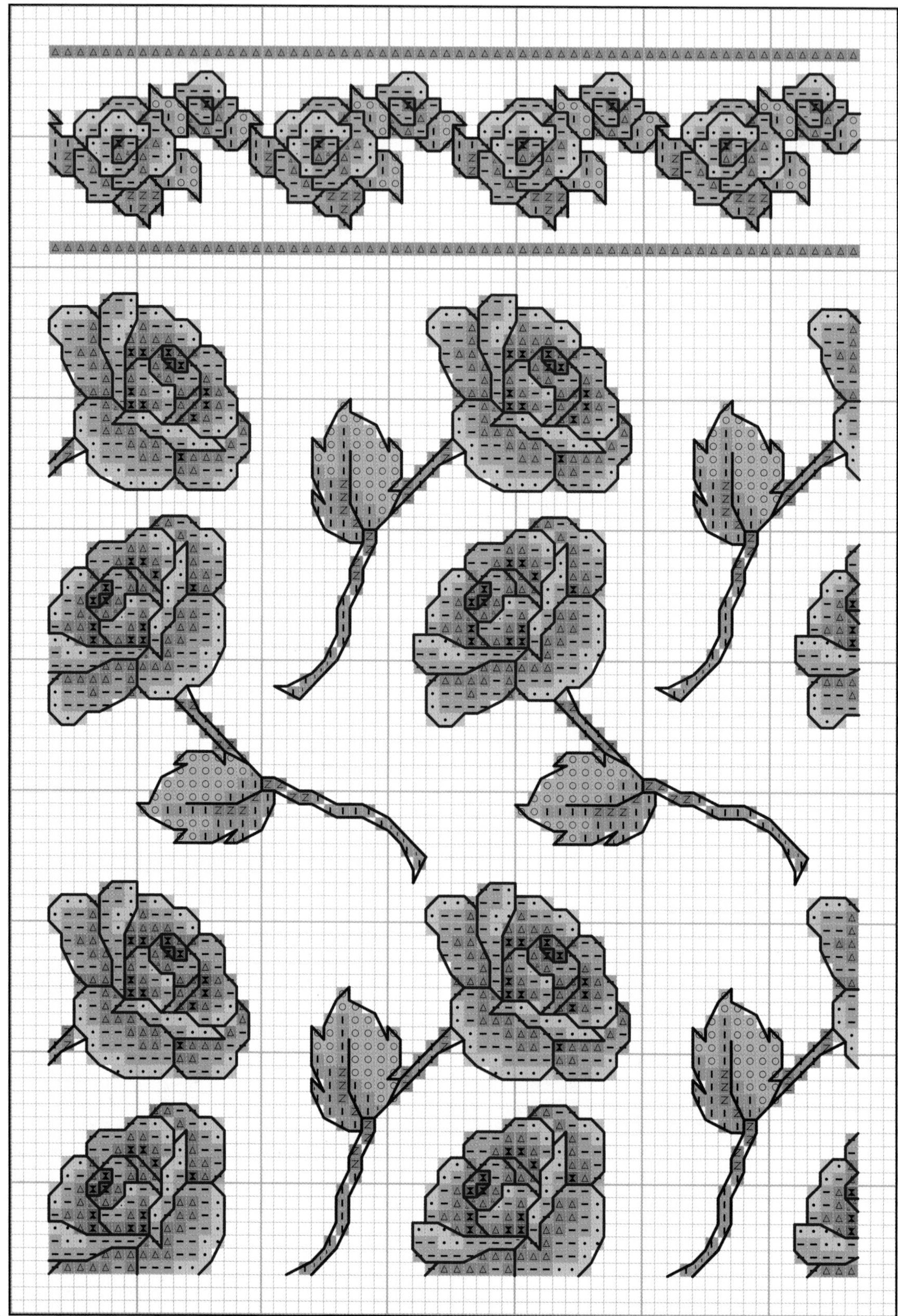

CREATIVE WORLD
DMC
Mouliné
Stranded Cotton Art. 117
150
151
3346
3347
3348
3731
3733
3685
3345

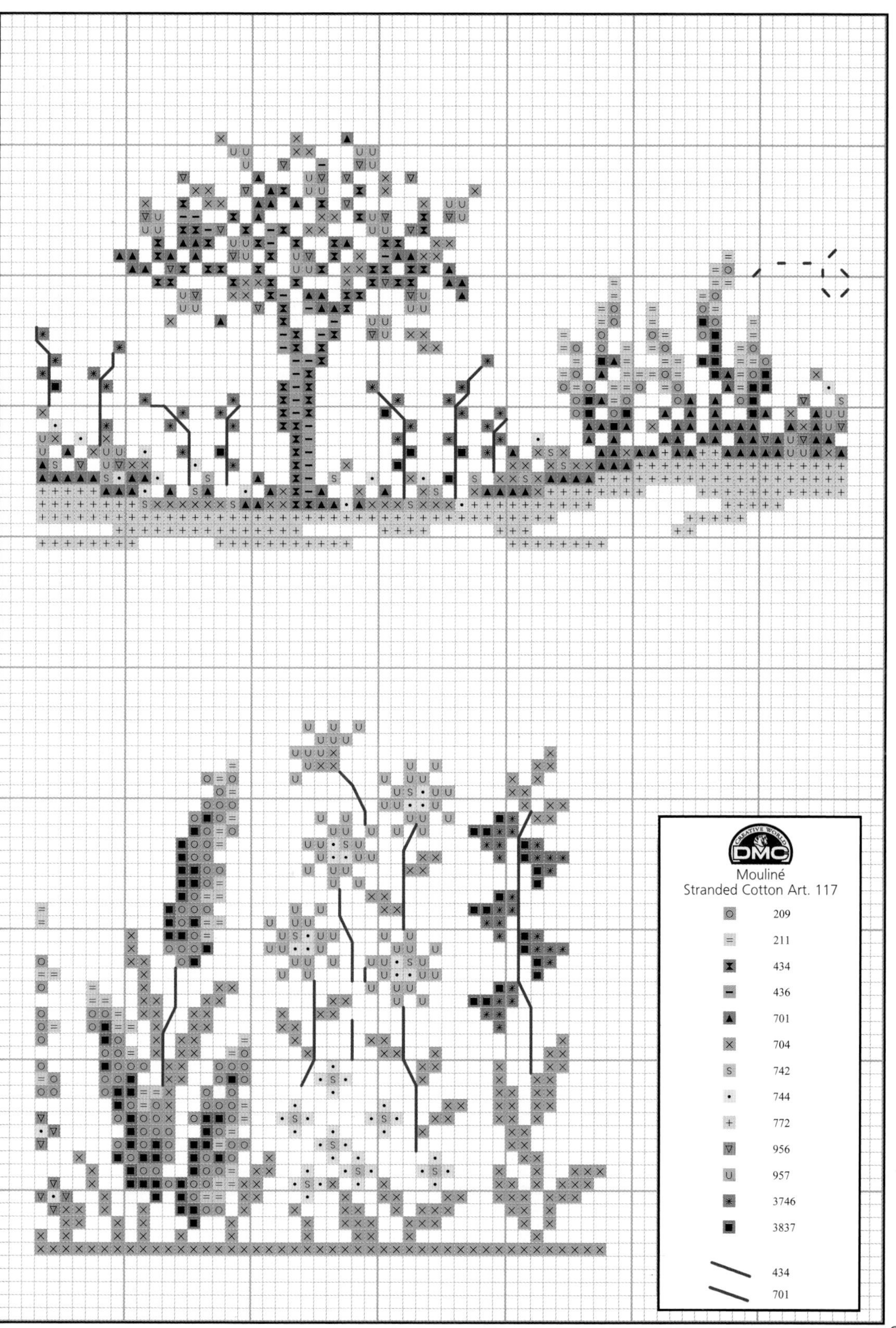
DMC
Mouliné
Stranded Cotton Art. 117
209
211
434
436
701
704
742
744
772
956
957
3746
3837
434
701

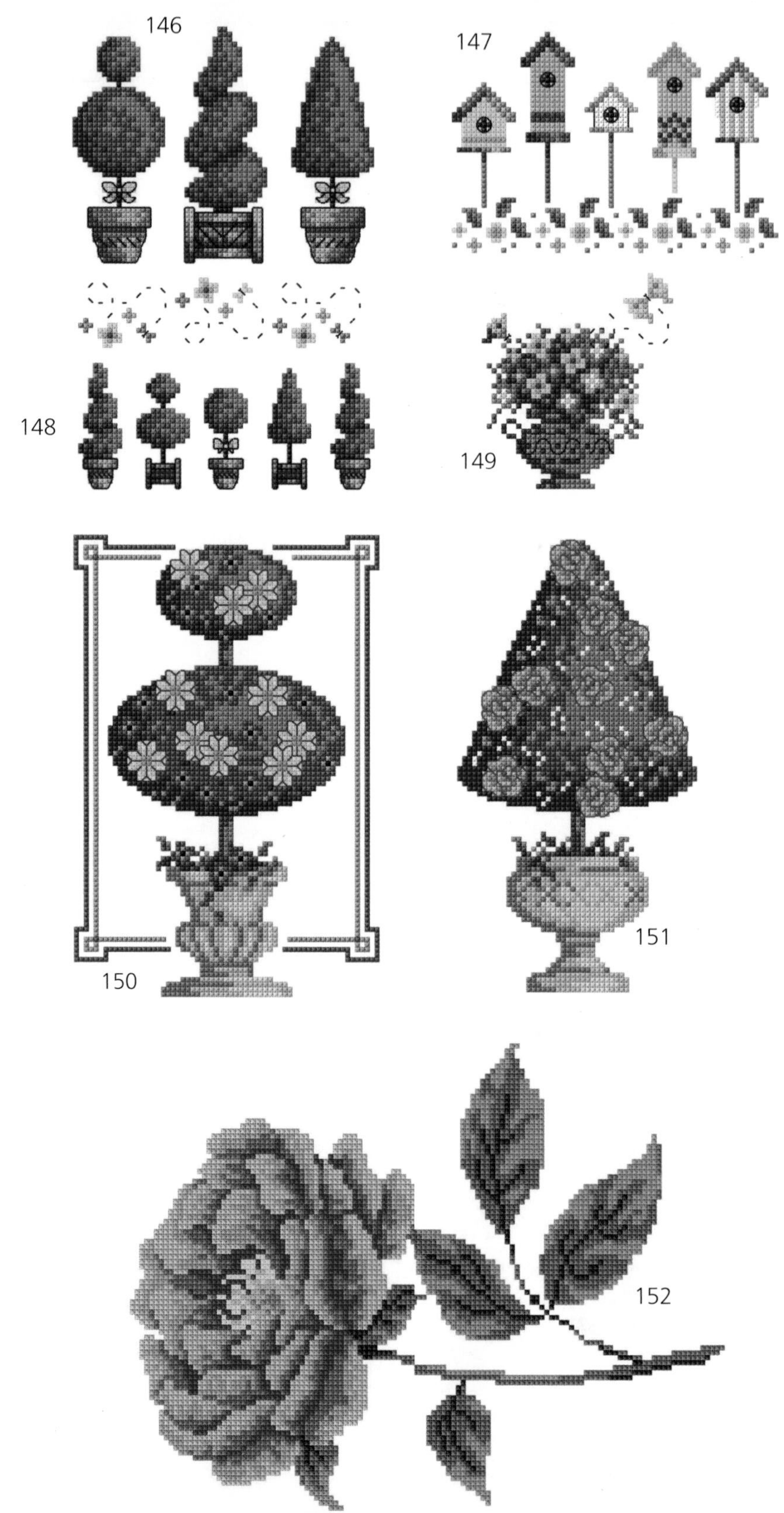
146
147
148
149
150
151
152

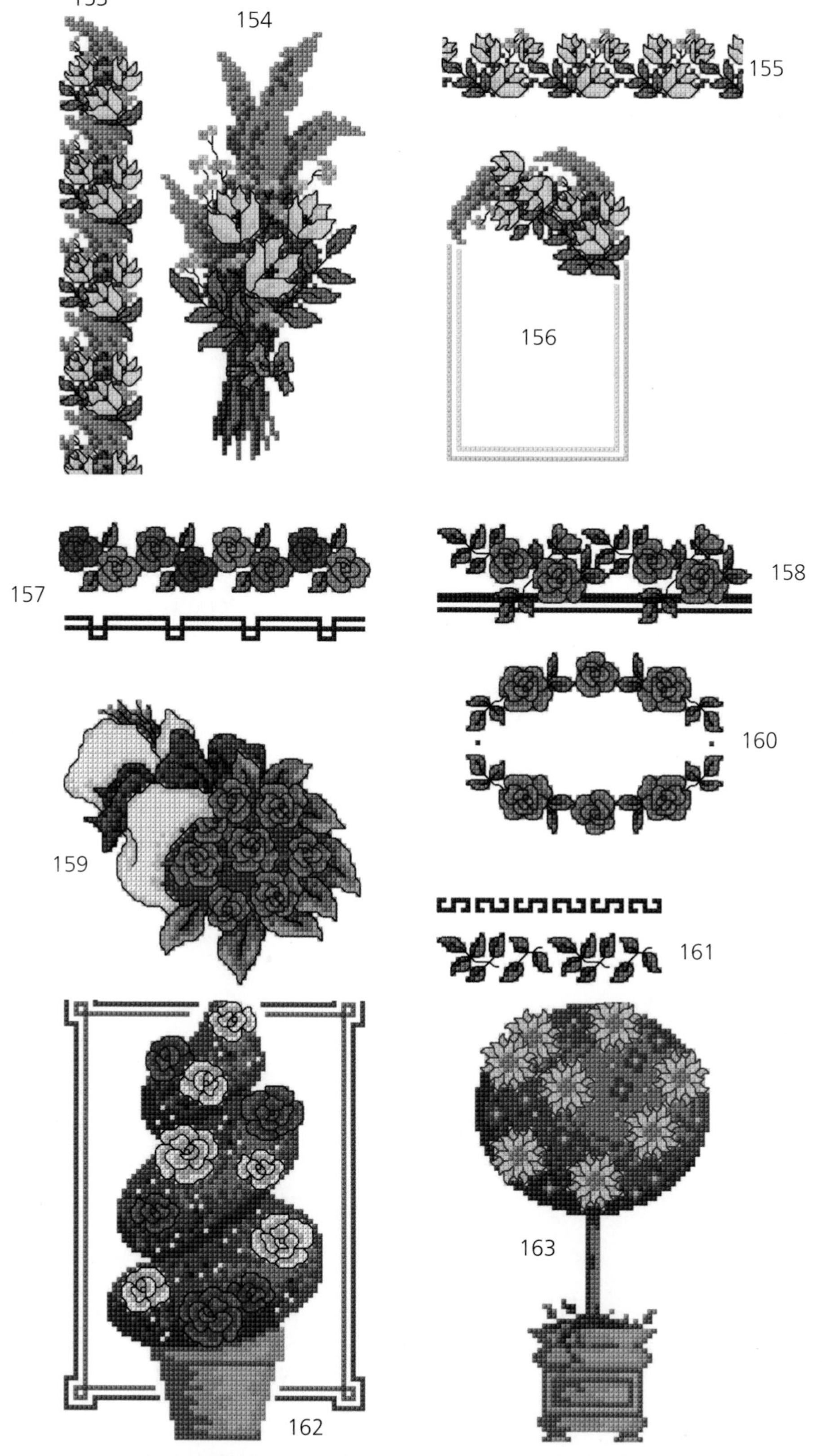
153
154
155
156
157
158
159
160
161
162
163

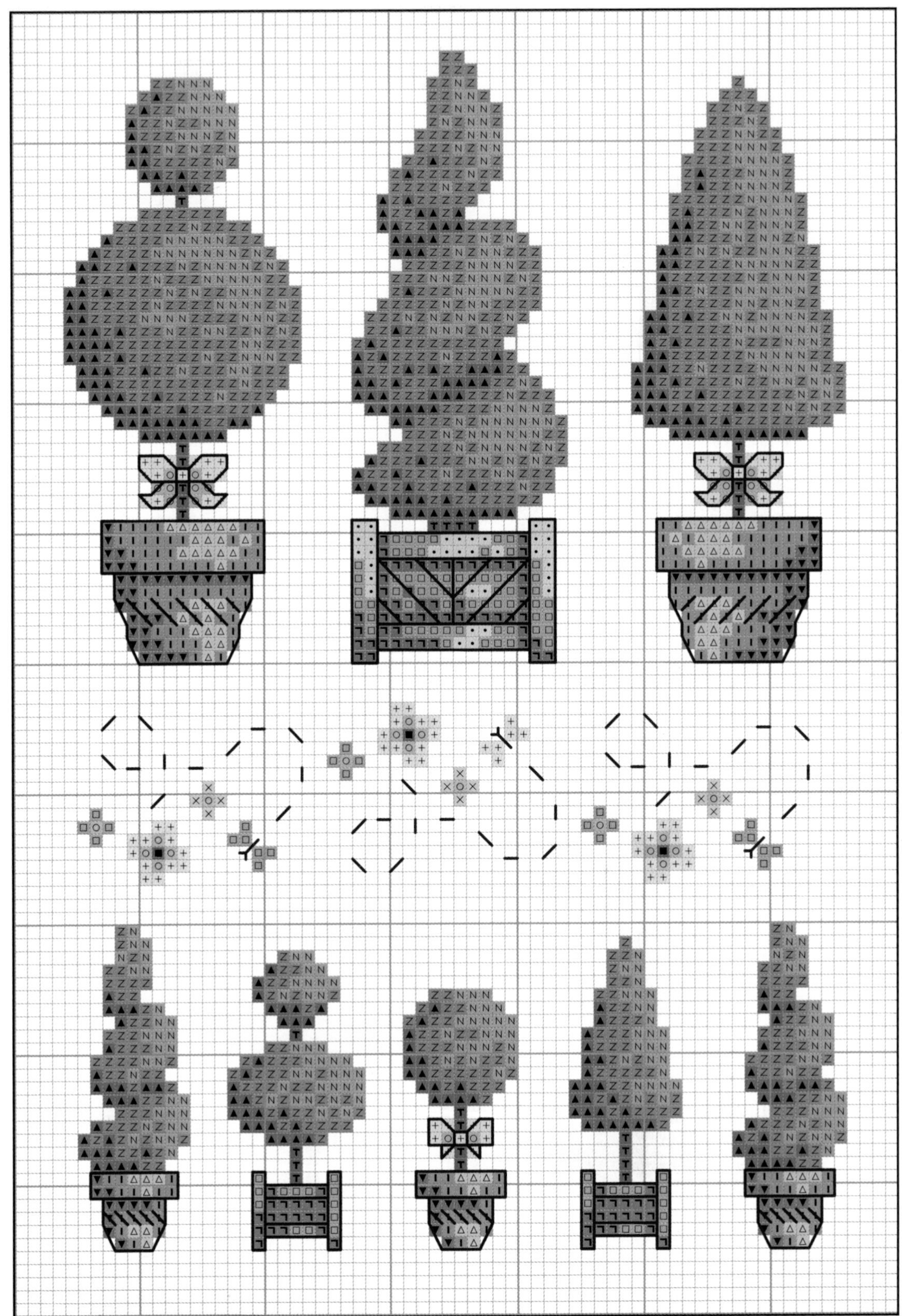

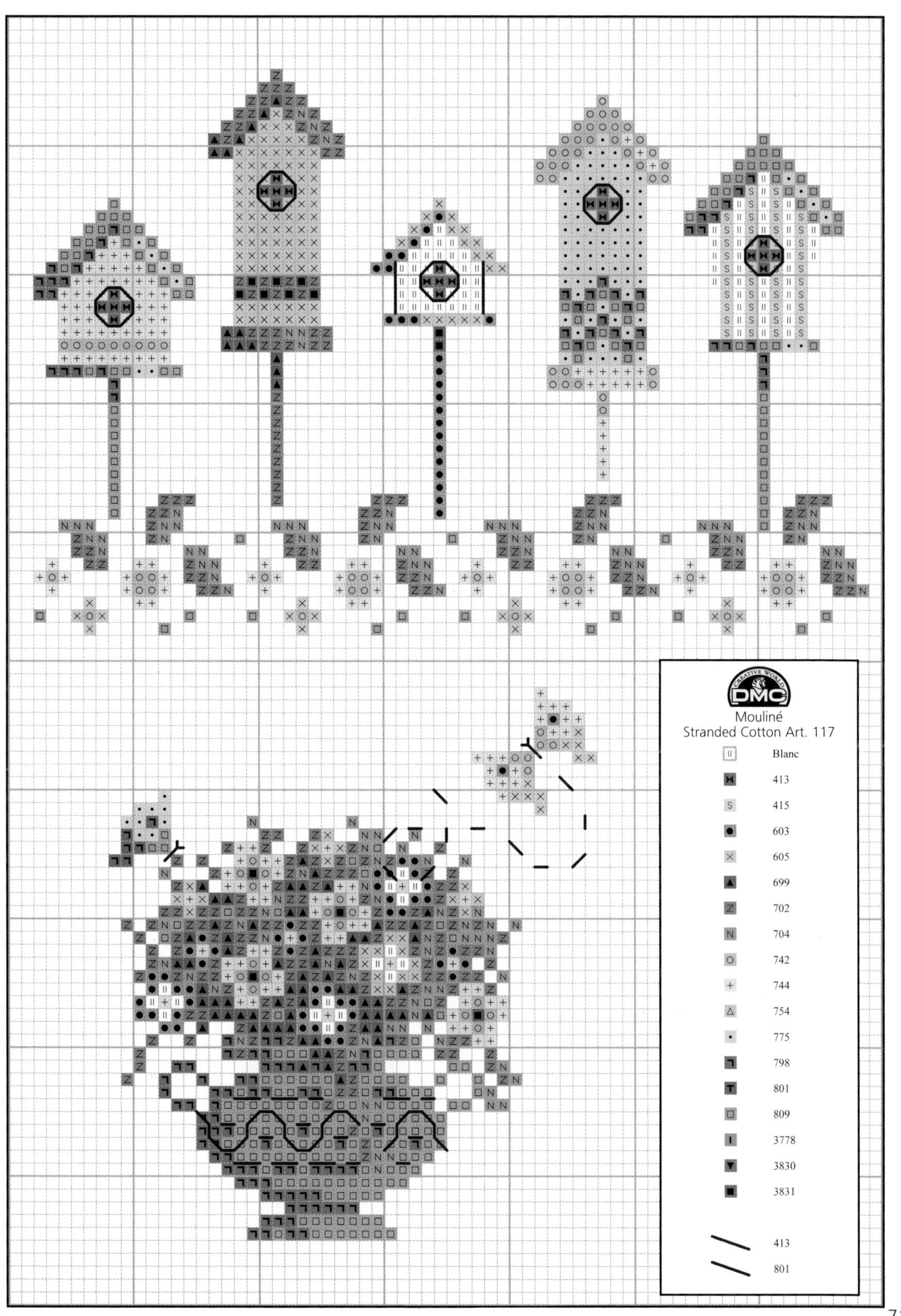
DMC
Mouliné
Stranded Cotton Art. 117
Blanc
413
415
603
605
699
702
704
742
744
754
775
798
801
809
3778
3830
3831
413
801

CREATIVE WORLD
DMC
Mouliné
Stranded Cotton Art. 117
Blanc
154
208
210
414
415
434
436
600
603
605
699
702
704
726
727
741
762
434
600

CREATIVE WORLD
DMC
Mouliné
Stranded Cotton Art. 117
Blanc
351
356
415
434
436
699
702
704
726
727
741
754
817
902
3771
434
902

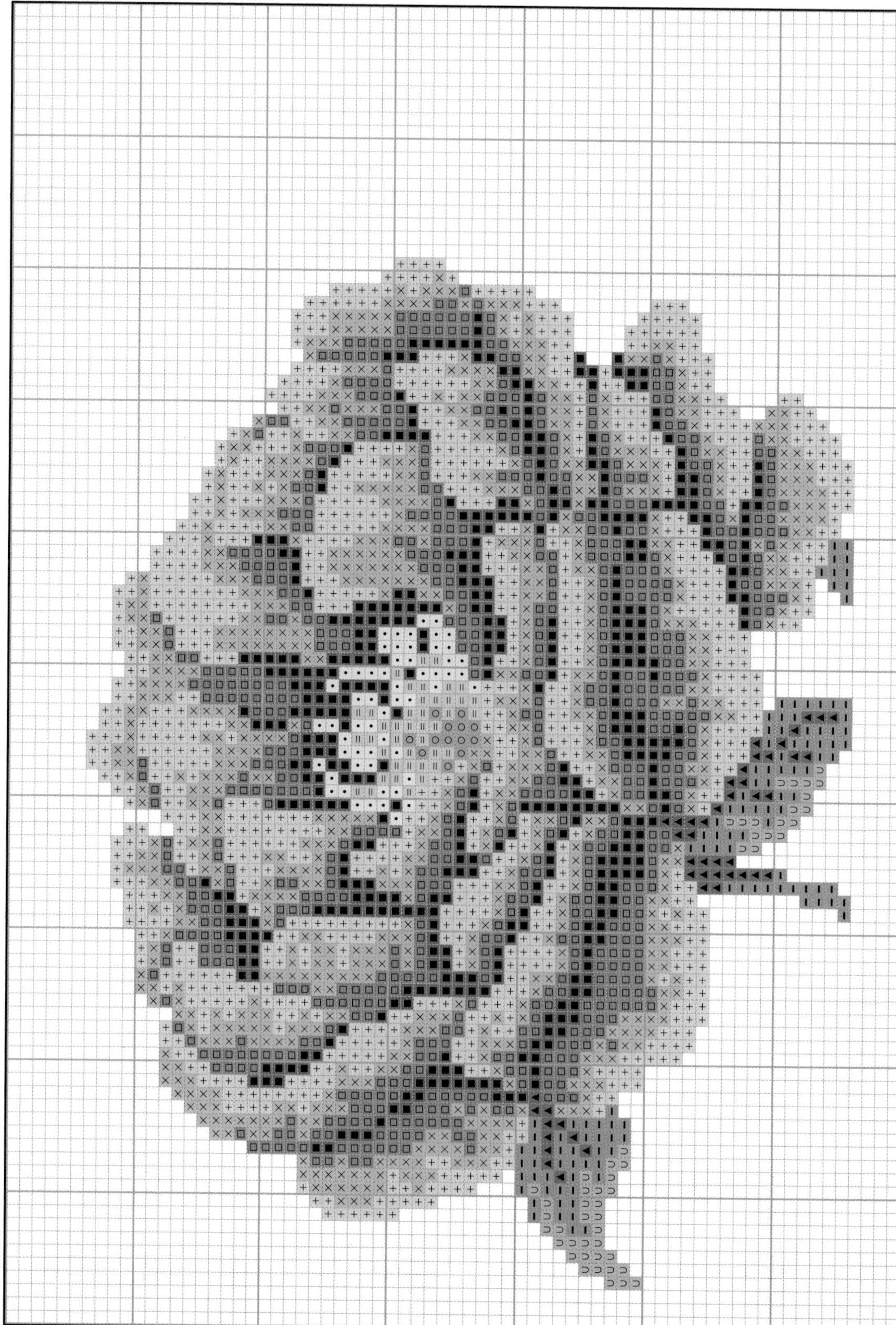

CREATIVE WORLD
DMC
Mouliné
Stranded Cotton Art. 117
326
602
604
725
727
783
963
3345
3347
3348

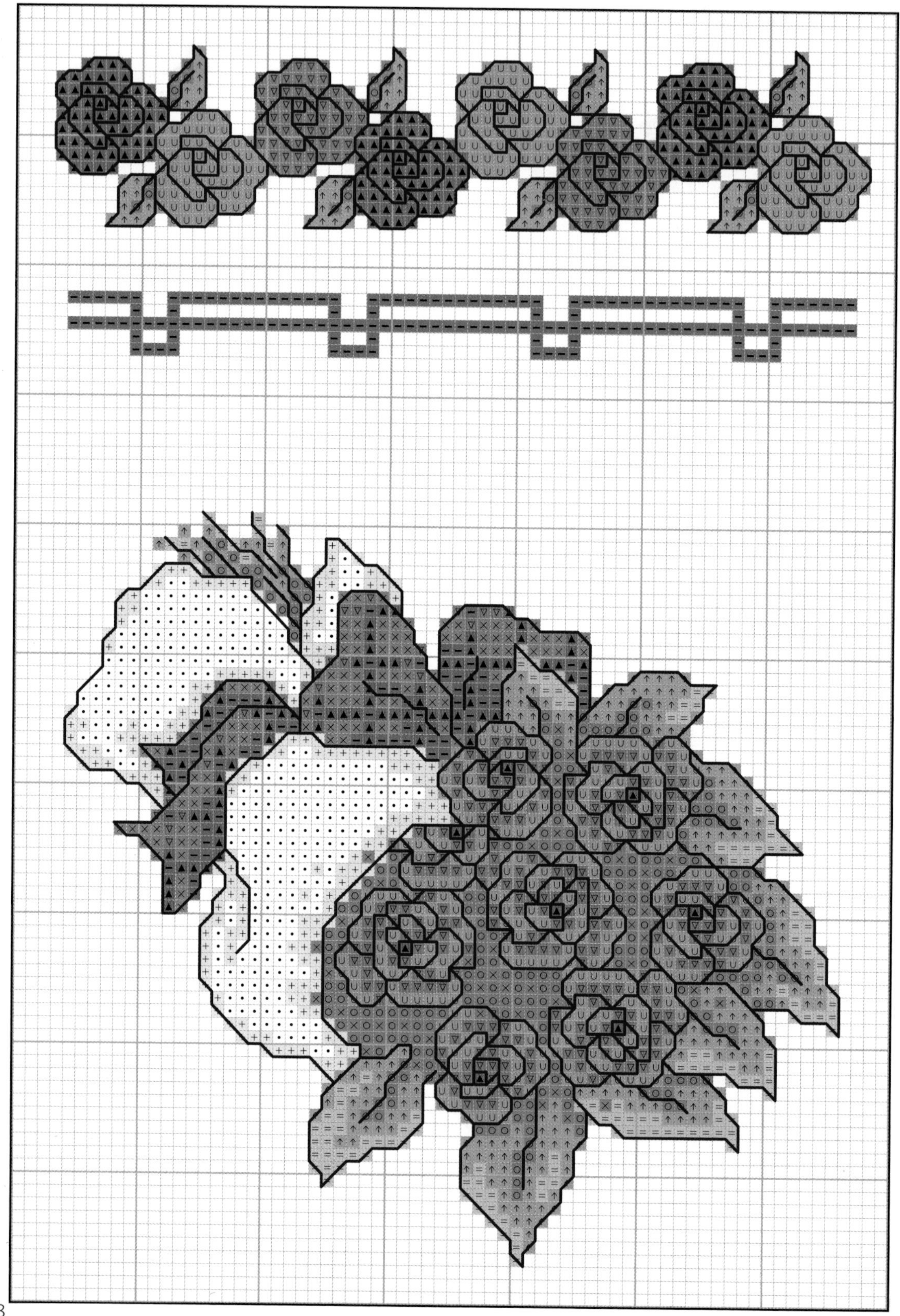

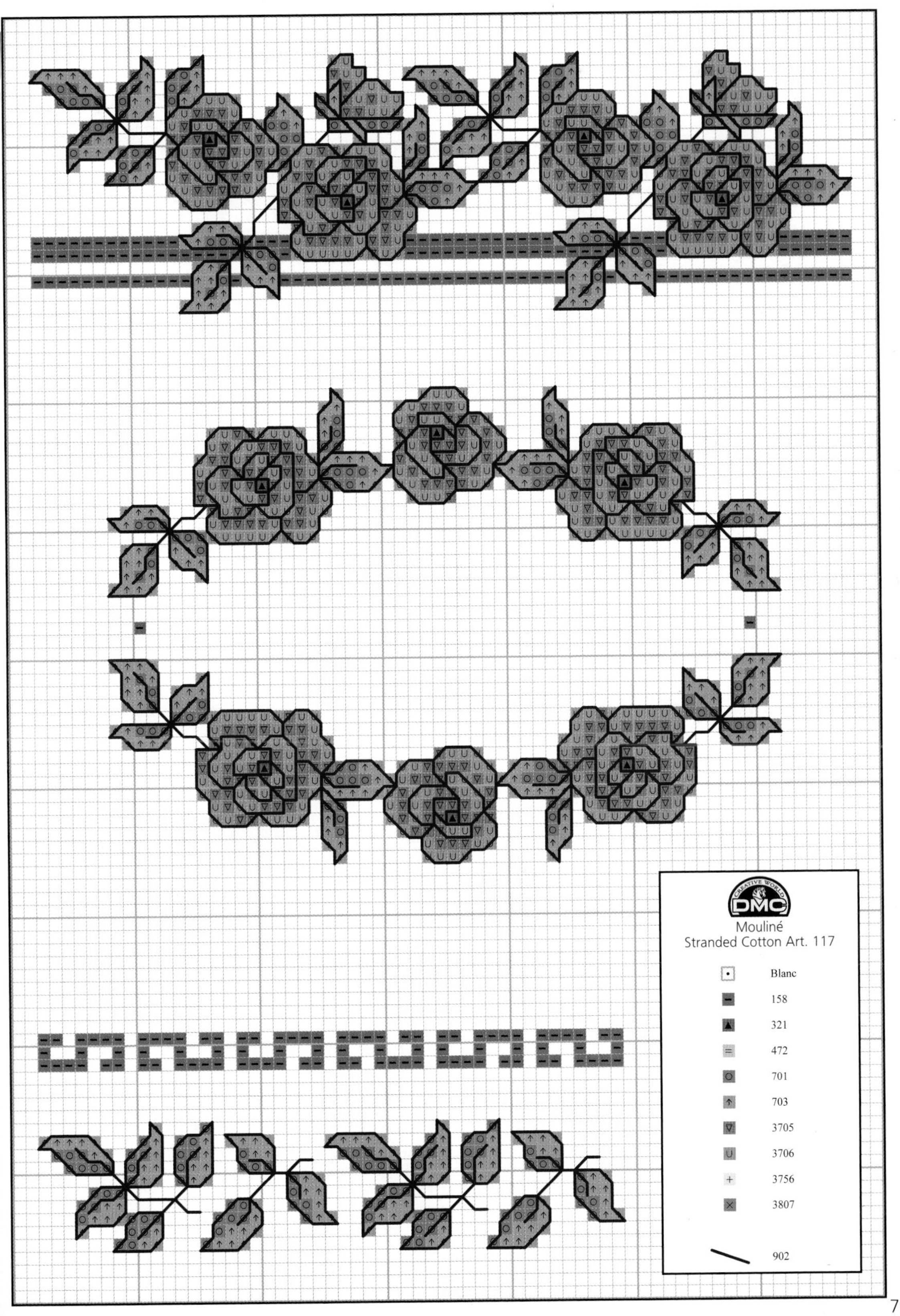
DMC
Mouliné
Stranded Cotton Art. 117
Blanc
158
321
472
701
703
3705
3706
3756
3807
902

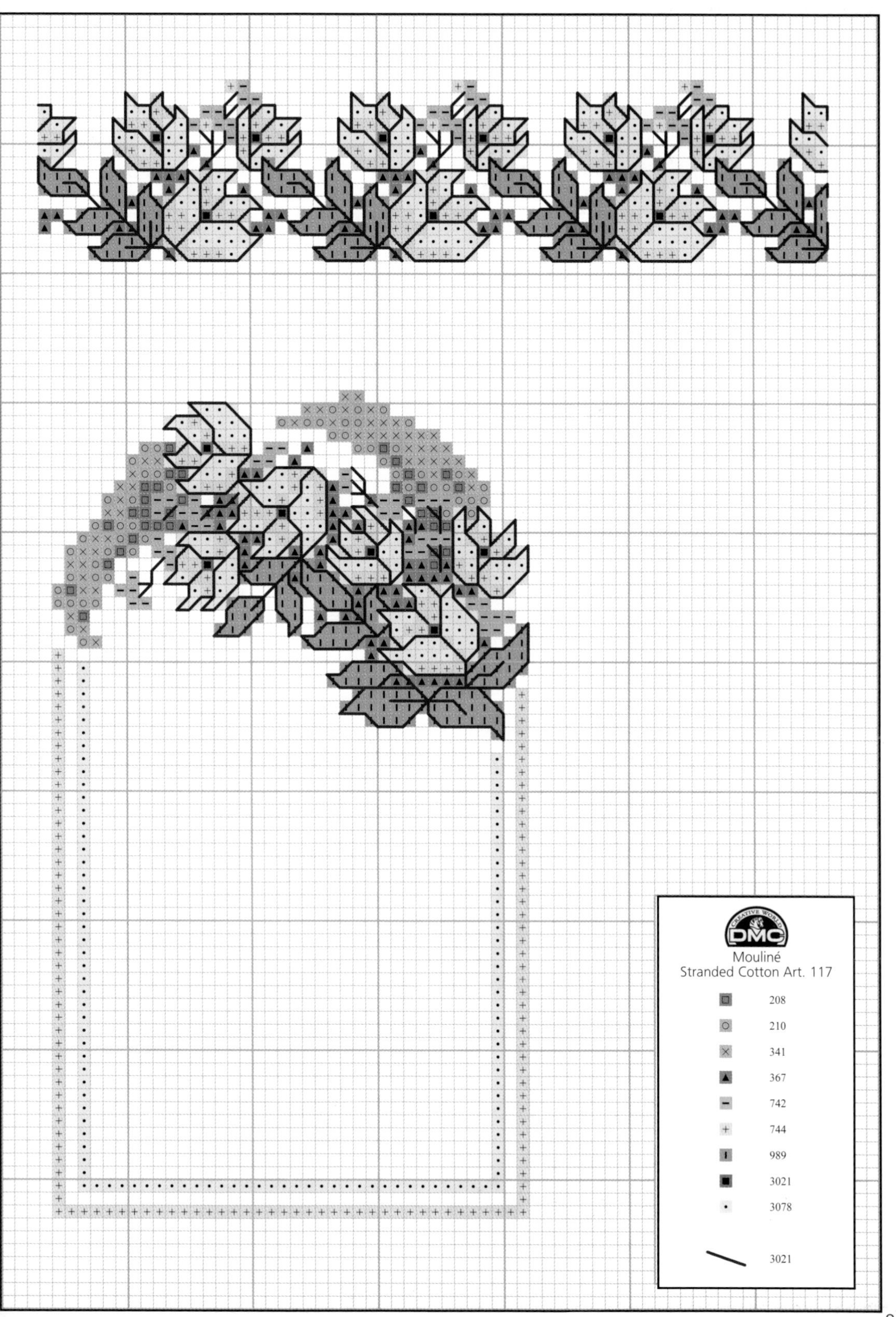
DMC
CREATIVE WORLD
Mouliné
Stranded Cotton Art. 117
208
210
341
367
742
744
989
3021
3078
3021

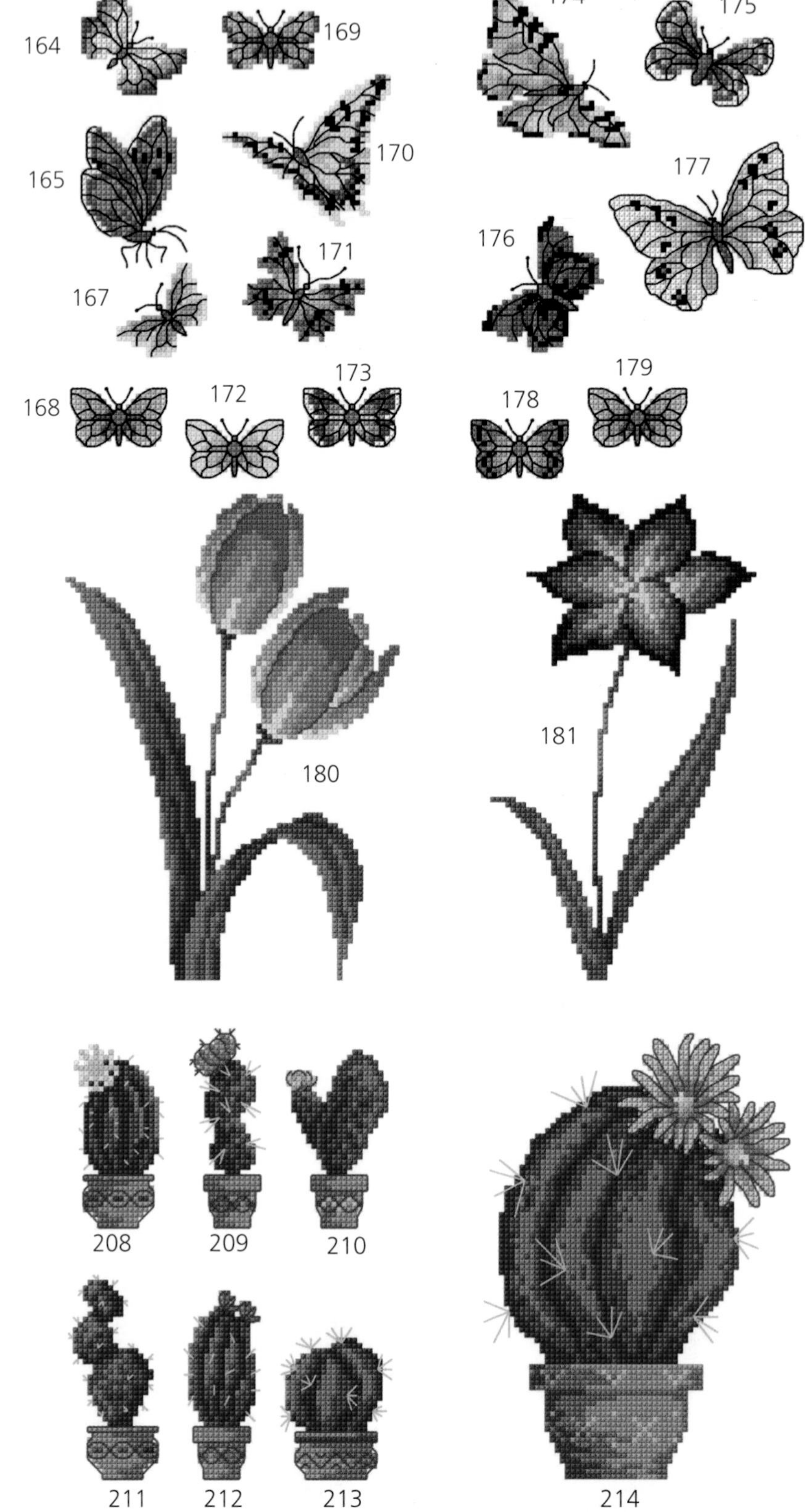
164
169
174
175
165
170
177
176
167
171
168
172
173
178
179
180
181
208
209
210
211
212
213
214

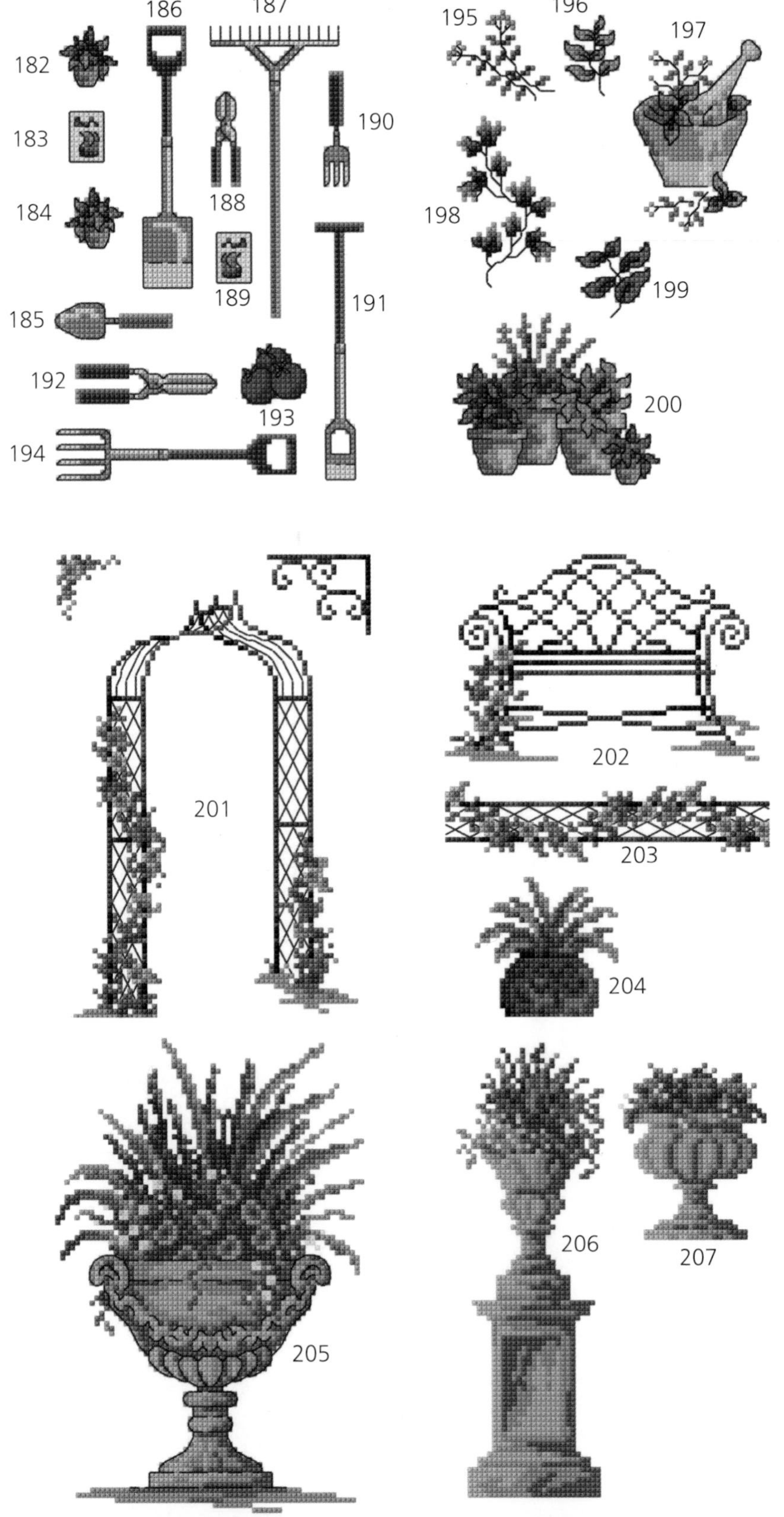
182
183
184
185
186
187
188
189
190
191
192
193
194
195
196
197
198
199
200
201
202
203
204
205
206
207

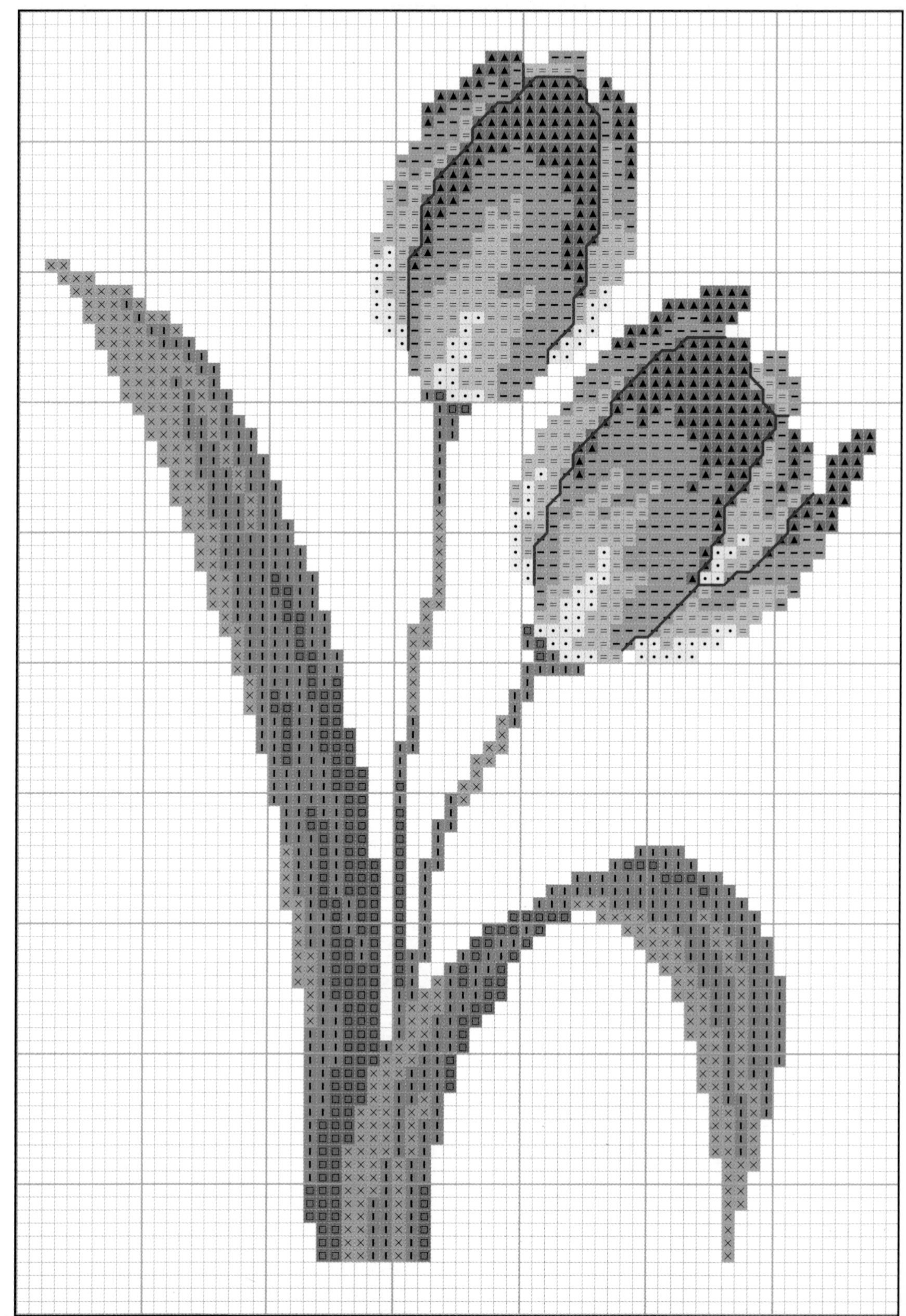

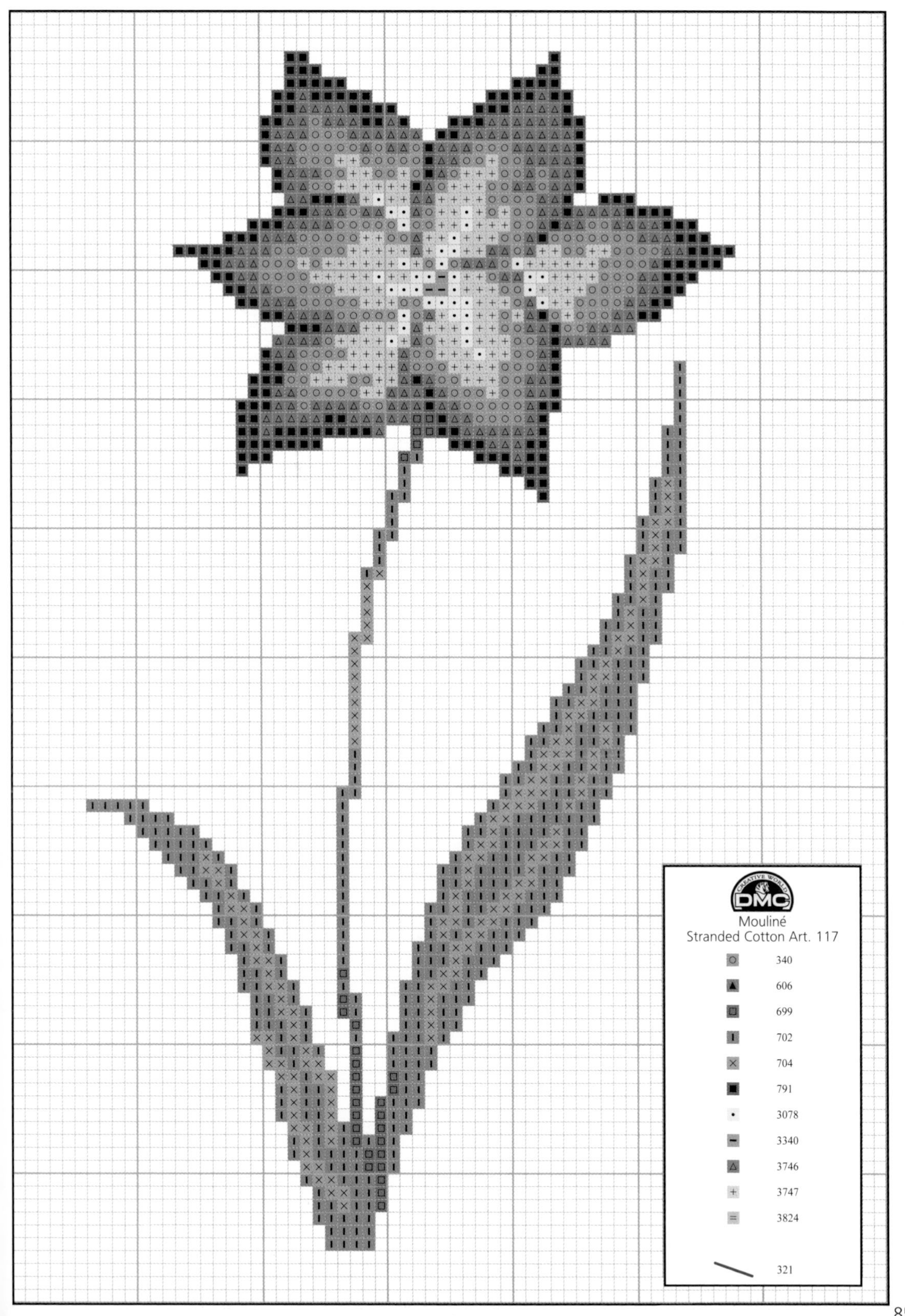
DMC
CREATIVE WORLD
Mouliné
Stranded Cotton Art. 117
340
606
699
702
704
791
3078
3340
3746
3747
3824
321

DMC
CREATIVE WORLD
Mouliné
Stranded Cotton Art. 117
699
702
704
726
742
818
956
957
3078
3350
3771
3778
165
3350

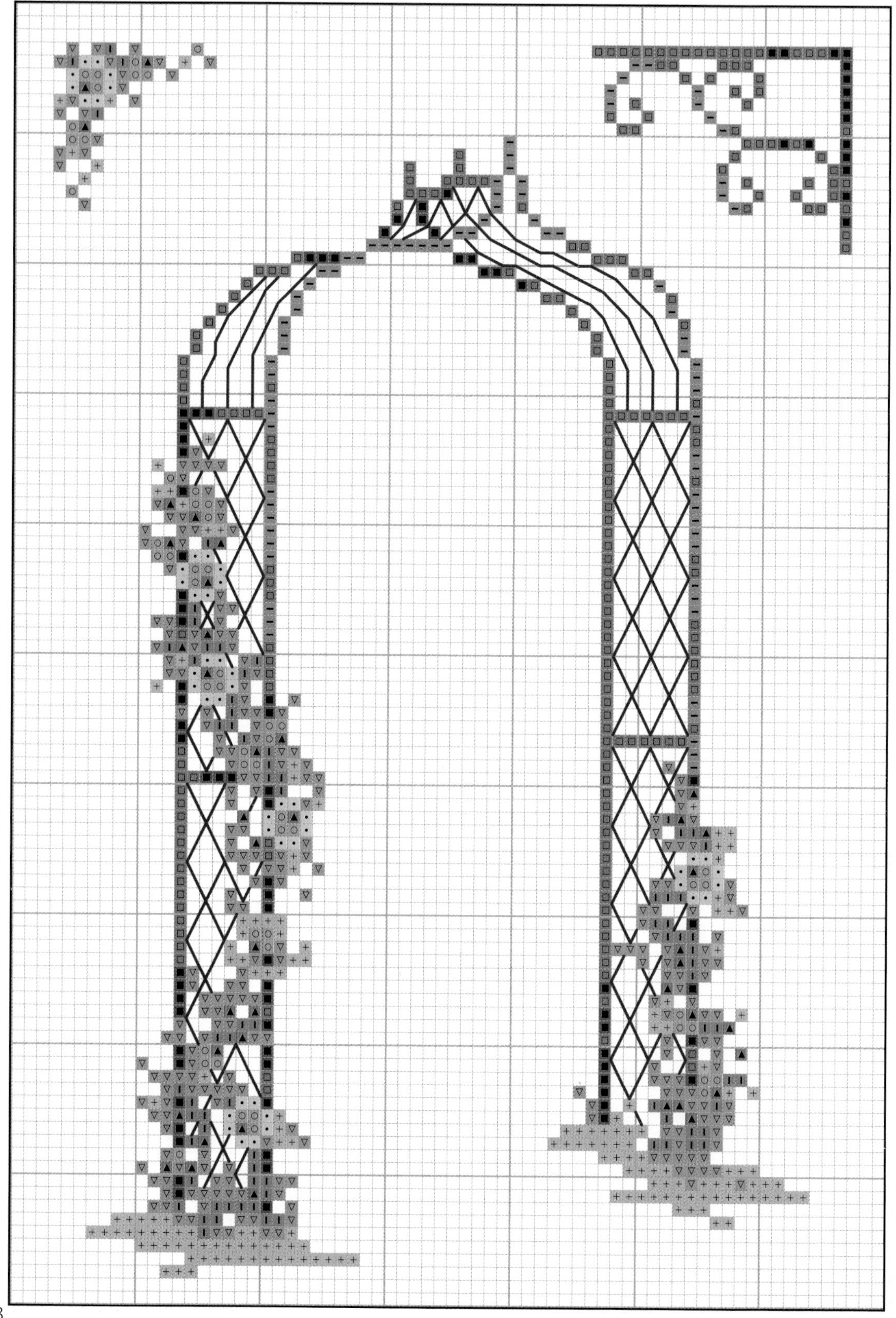

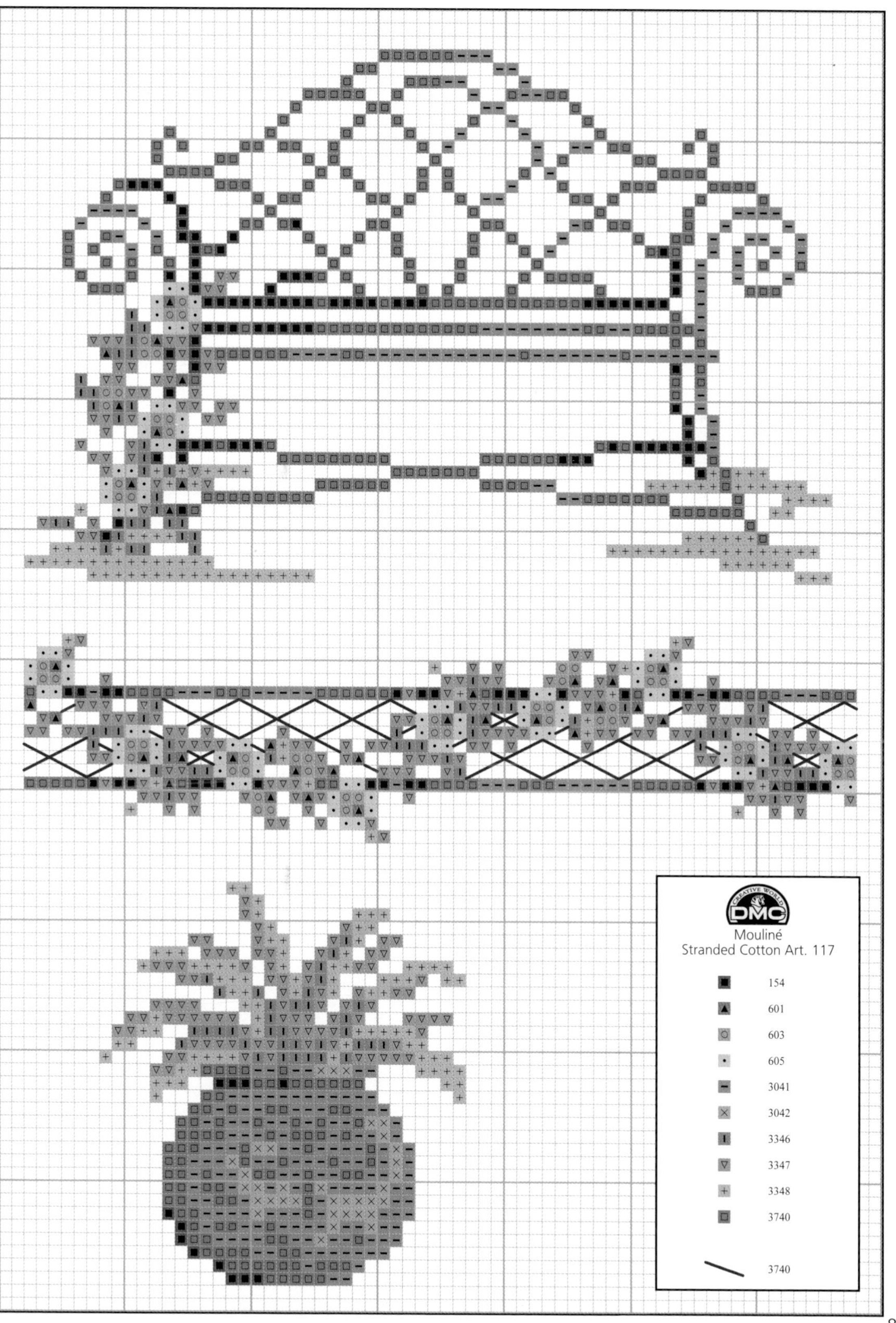
DMC
CREATIVE WORLD
Mouliné
Stranded Cotton Art. 117
154
601
603
605
3041
3042
3346
3347
3348
3740
3740

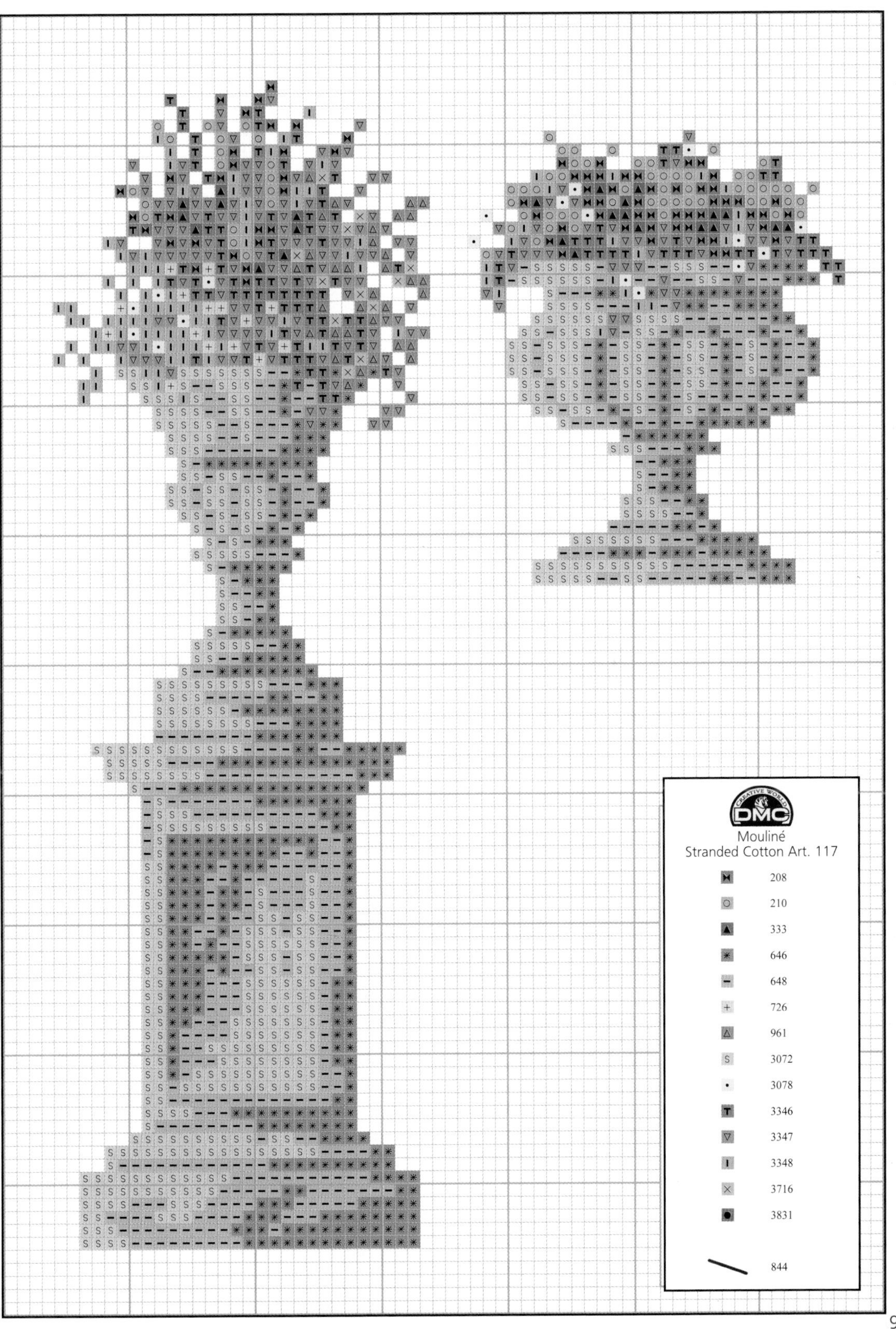
DMC
Mouliné
Stranded Cotton Art. 117
208
210
333
646
648
726
961
3072
3078
3346
3347
3348
3716
3831
844

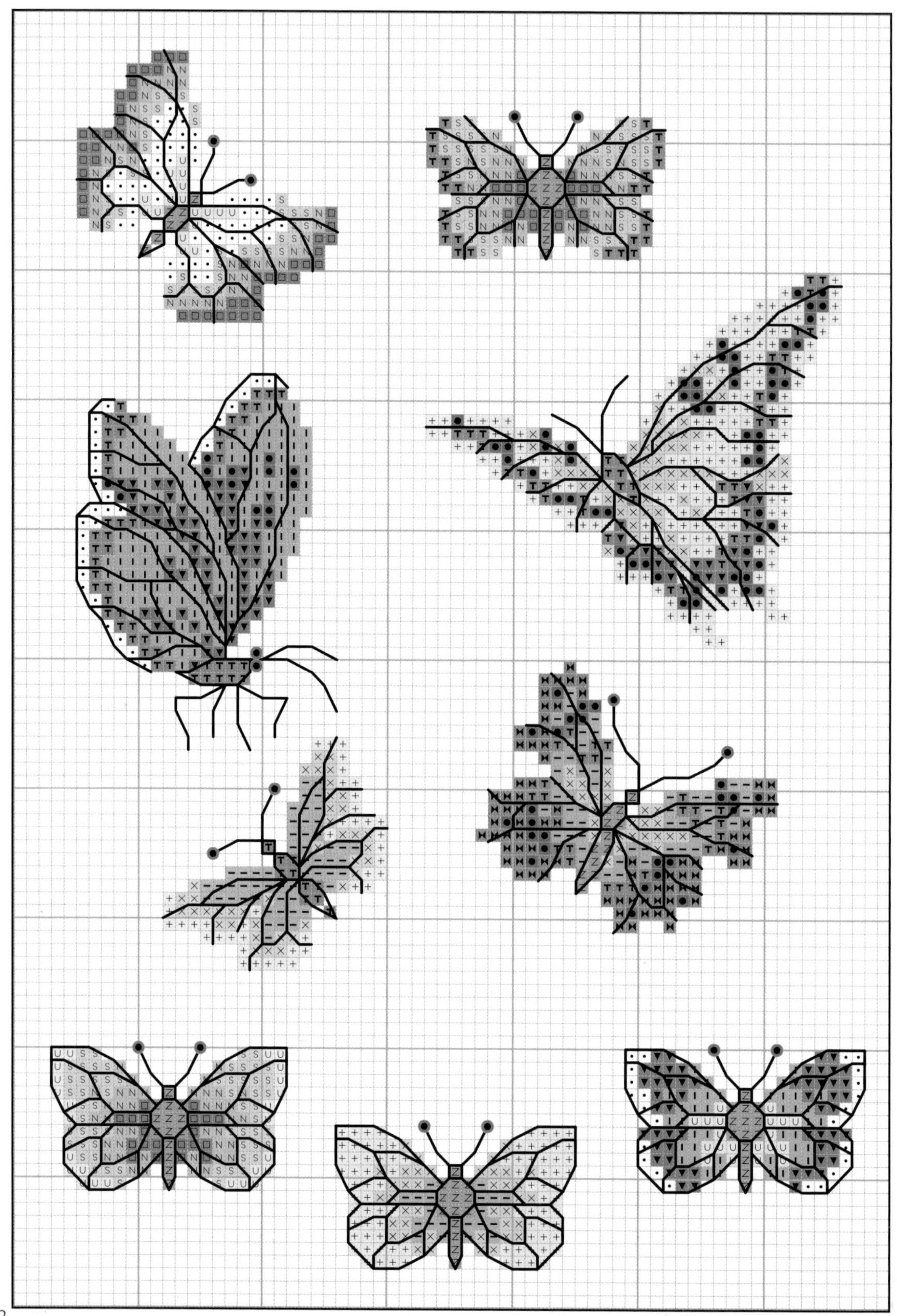

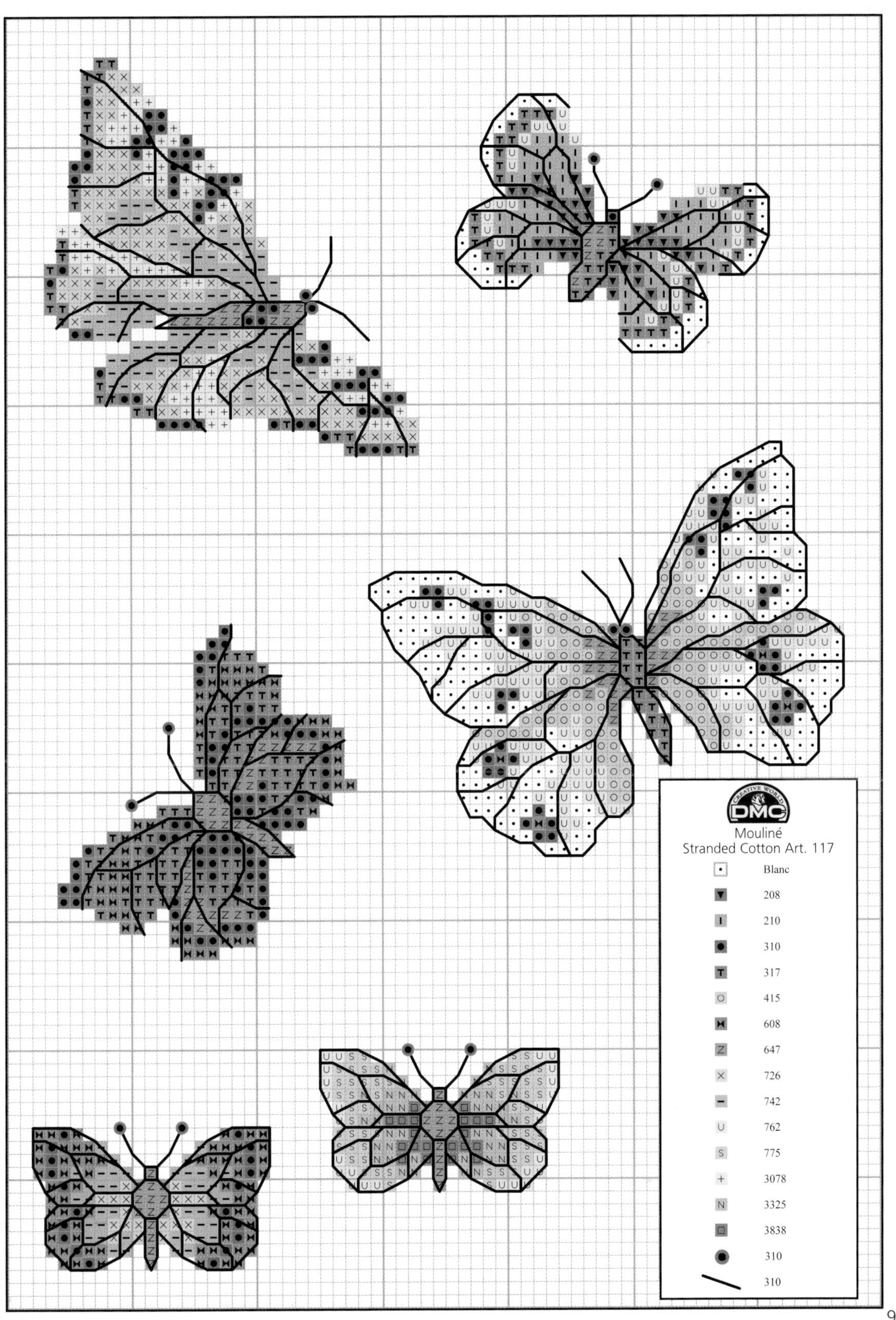
DMC
CREATIVE WORLD
Mouliné
Stranded Cotton Art. 117
Blanc
208
210
310
317
415
608
647
726
742
762
775
3078
3325
3838
310
310

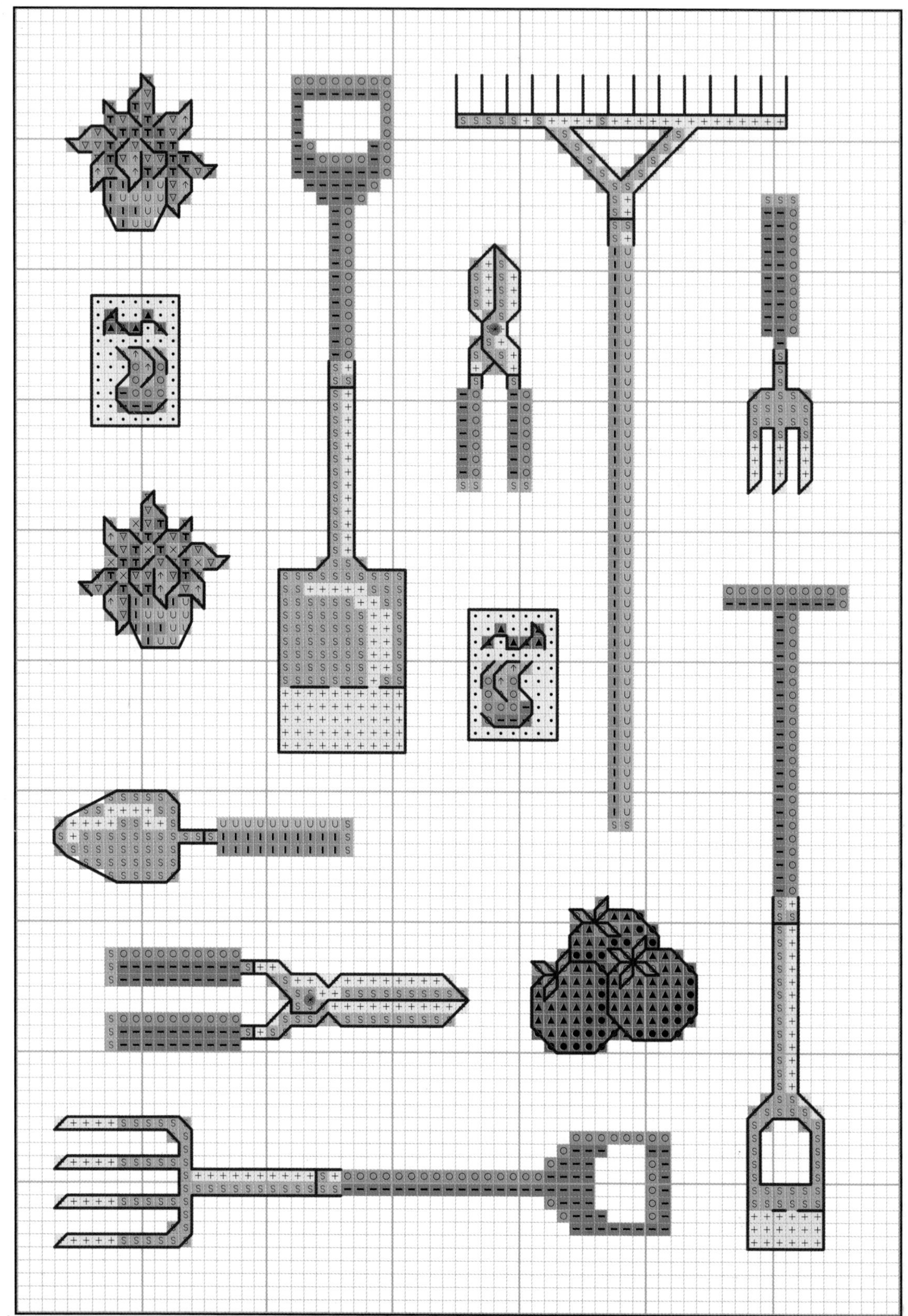

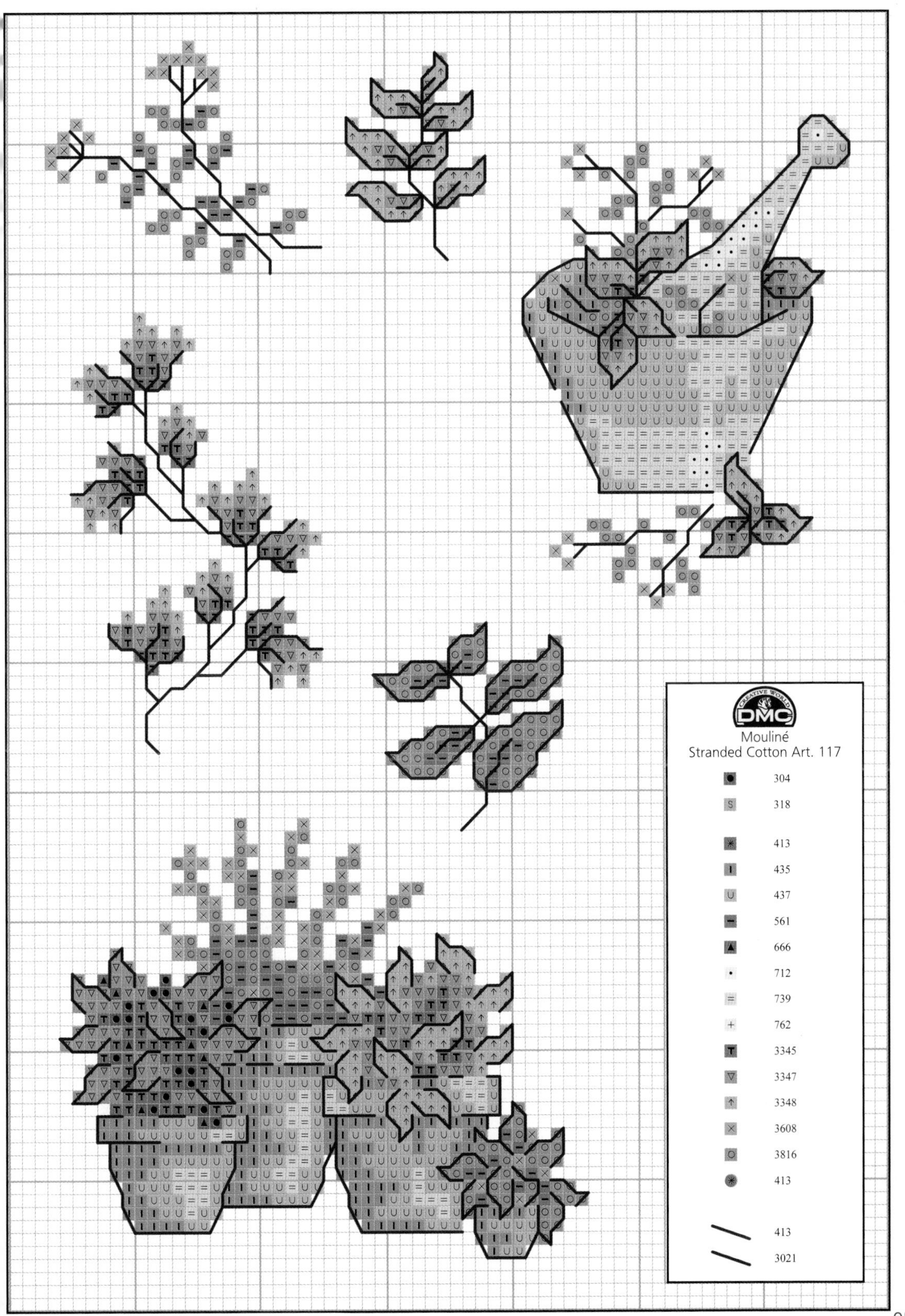
DMC
Mouliné
Stranded Cotton Art. 117
304
318
413
435
437
561
666
712
739
762
3345
3347
3348
3608
3816
413
413
3021

215 216

Aa Bb Cc Çç Dd Ee
Ff Gg Ğğ Hh Iı İi Jj
Kk Ll Mm Nn Oo
Öö Pp Qq Rr Ss Şş
Tt Uu Üü Vv Ww
Xx Yy Zz

Aa Bb Cc Çç Dd Ee Ff Gg
Ğğ Hh Iı İi Jj Kk Ll Mm Nn
Oo Öö Pp Qq Rr Ss Şş Tt
Uu Üü Vv Ww Xx Yy Zz

ABCÇDEFGĞHIIJK
LMNOÖPQRSŞTUÜ
VWXYZ 0123456789

Aa Bb Cc Çç Dd Ee
Ff Gg Ğğ Hh Iı İi Jj
Kk Ll Mm Nn Oo Öö
Pp Qq Rr Ss Şş Tt
Uu Üü Vv W
w Xx Yy Zz

217

218

219

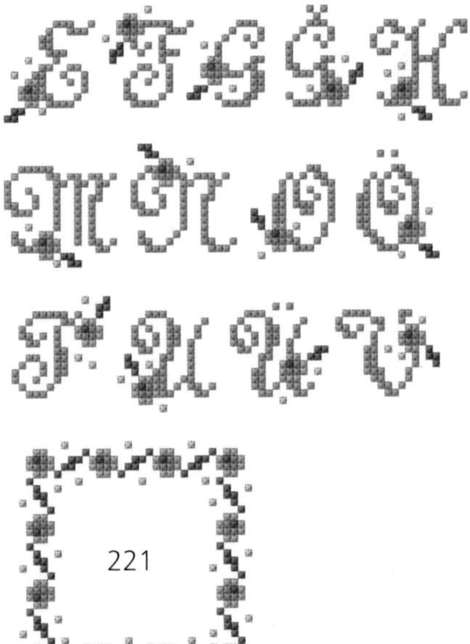

220

221

DMC
CREATIVE WORLD
Mouliné
Stranded Cotton Art. 117
3831
603
605
727
703
3831

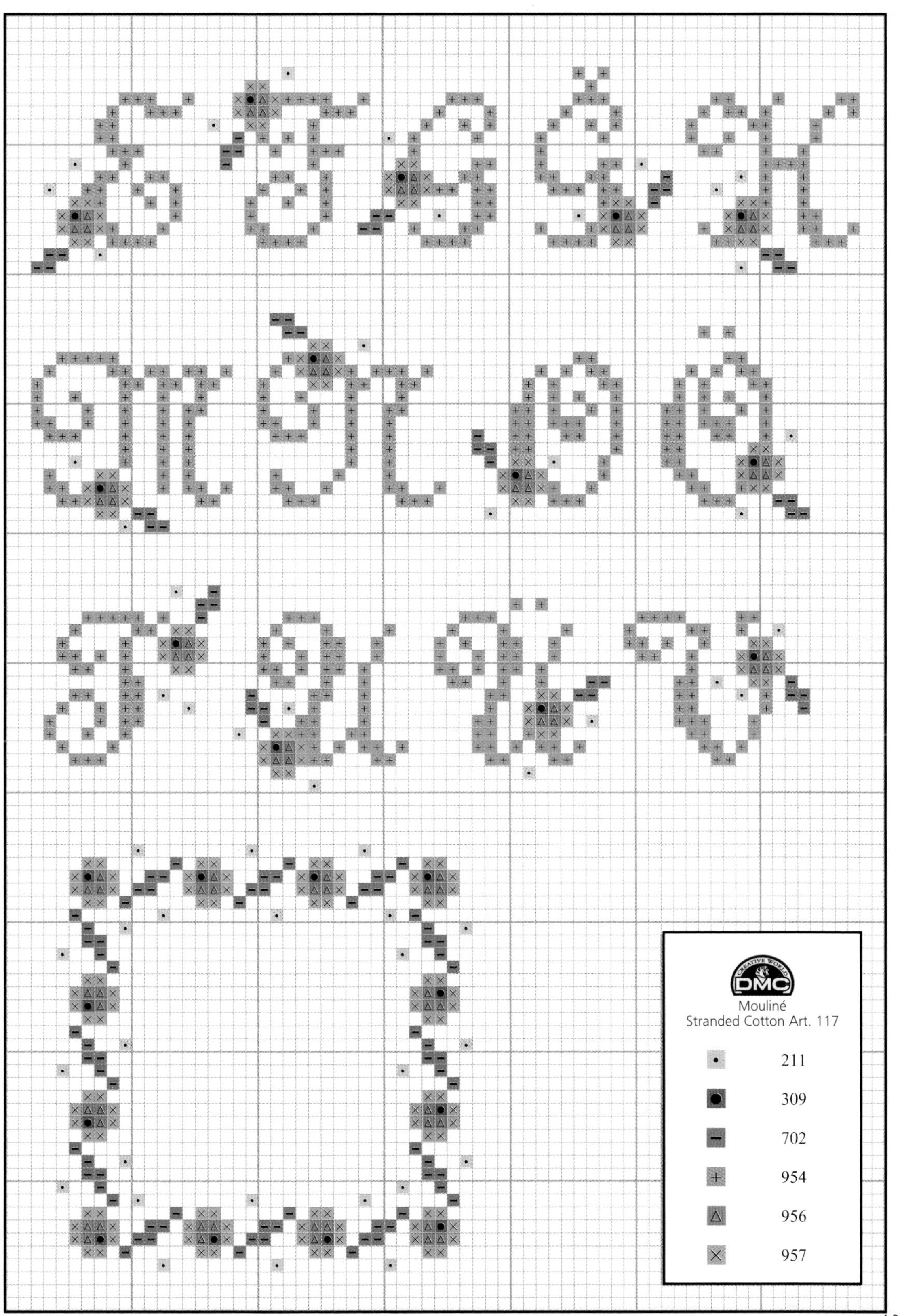

DMC
CREATIVE WORLD
Mouliné
Stranded Cotton Art. 117
211
309
702
954
956
957

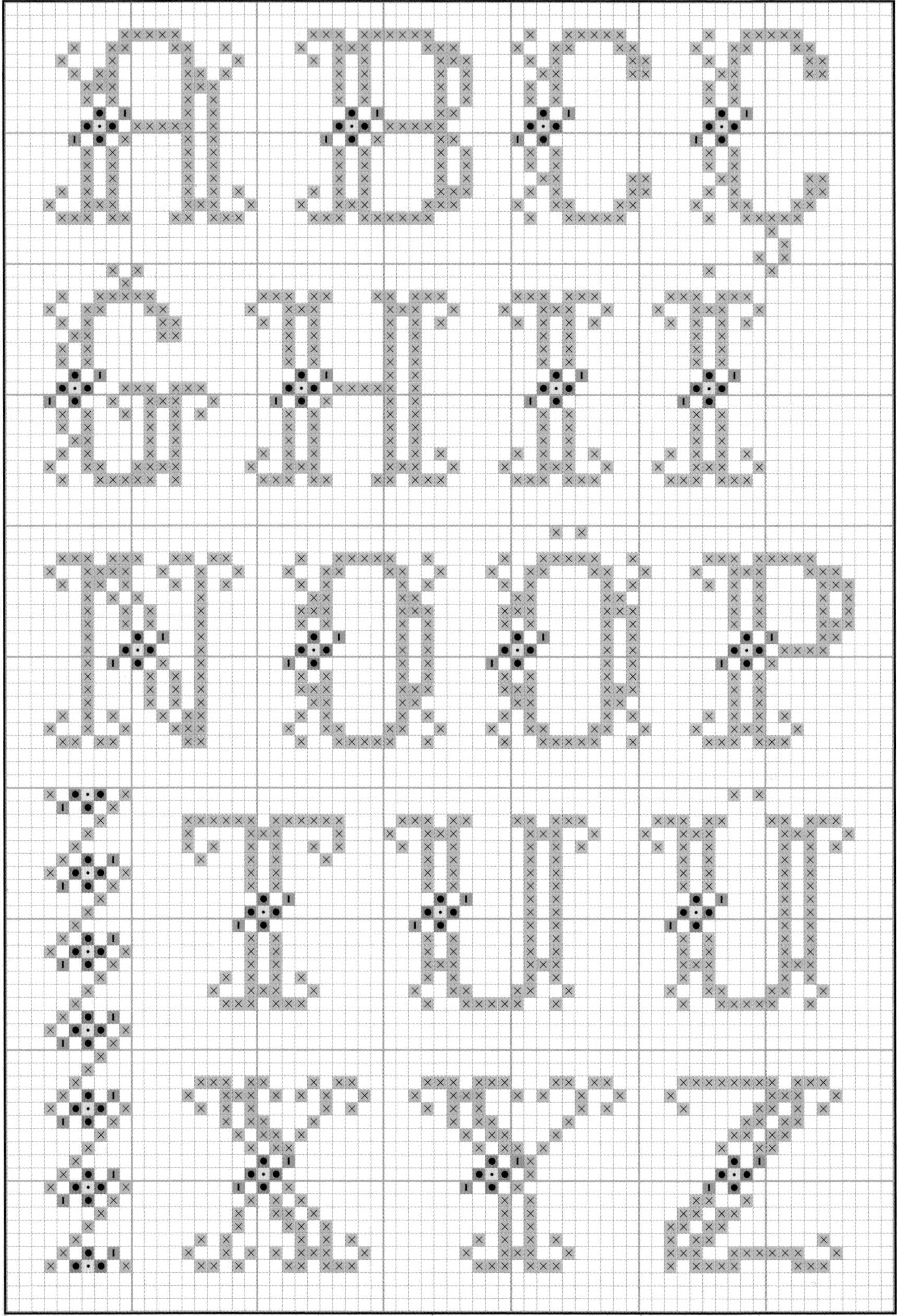

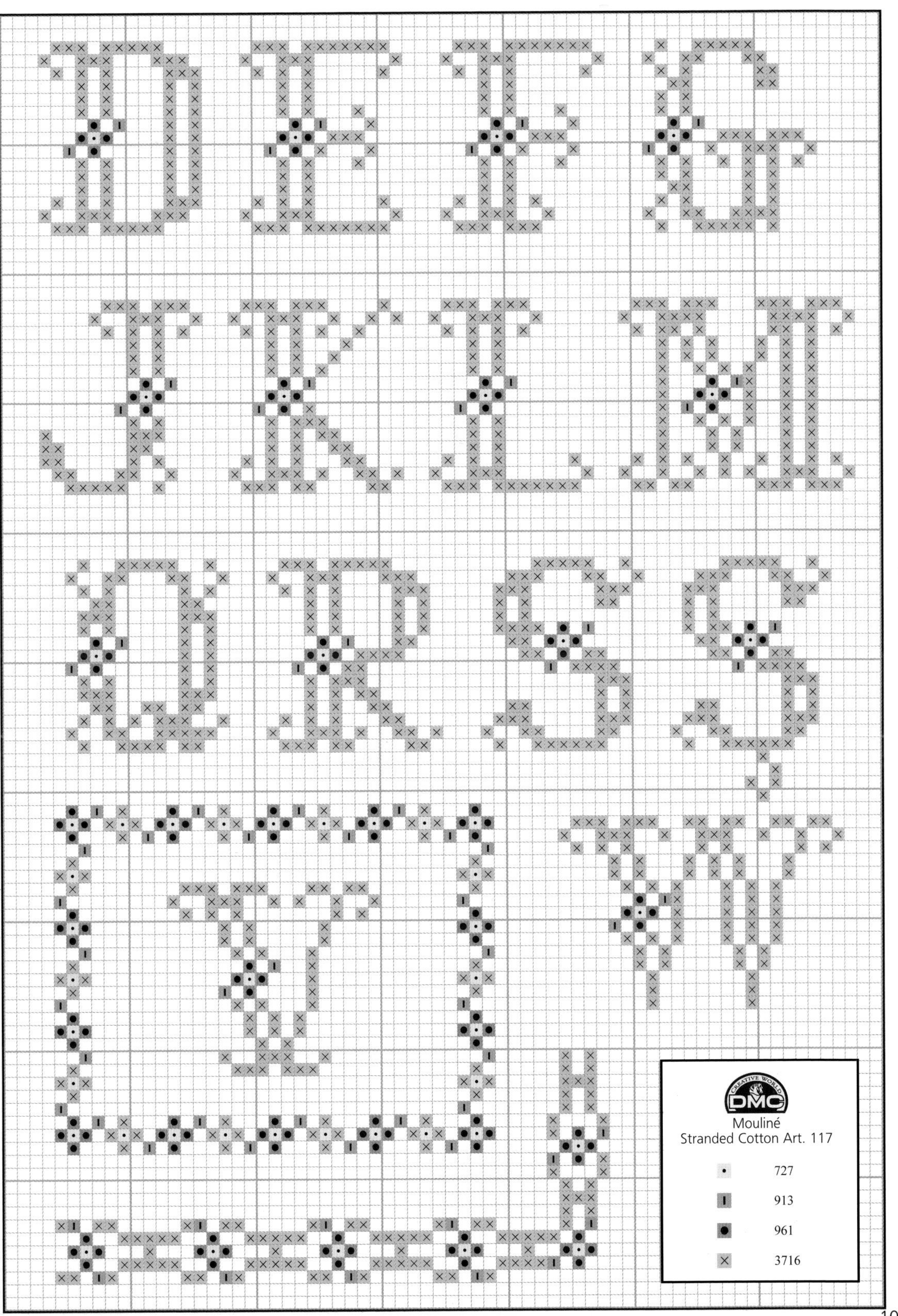
DMC
CREATIVE WORLD
Mouliné
Stranded Cotton Art. 117
727
913
961
3716

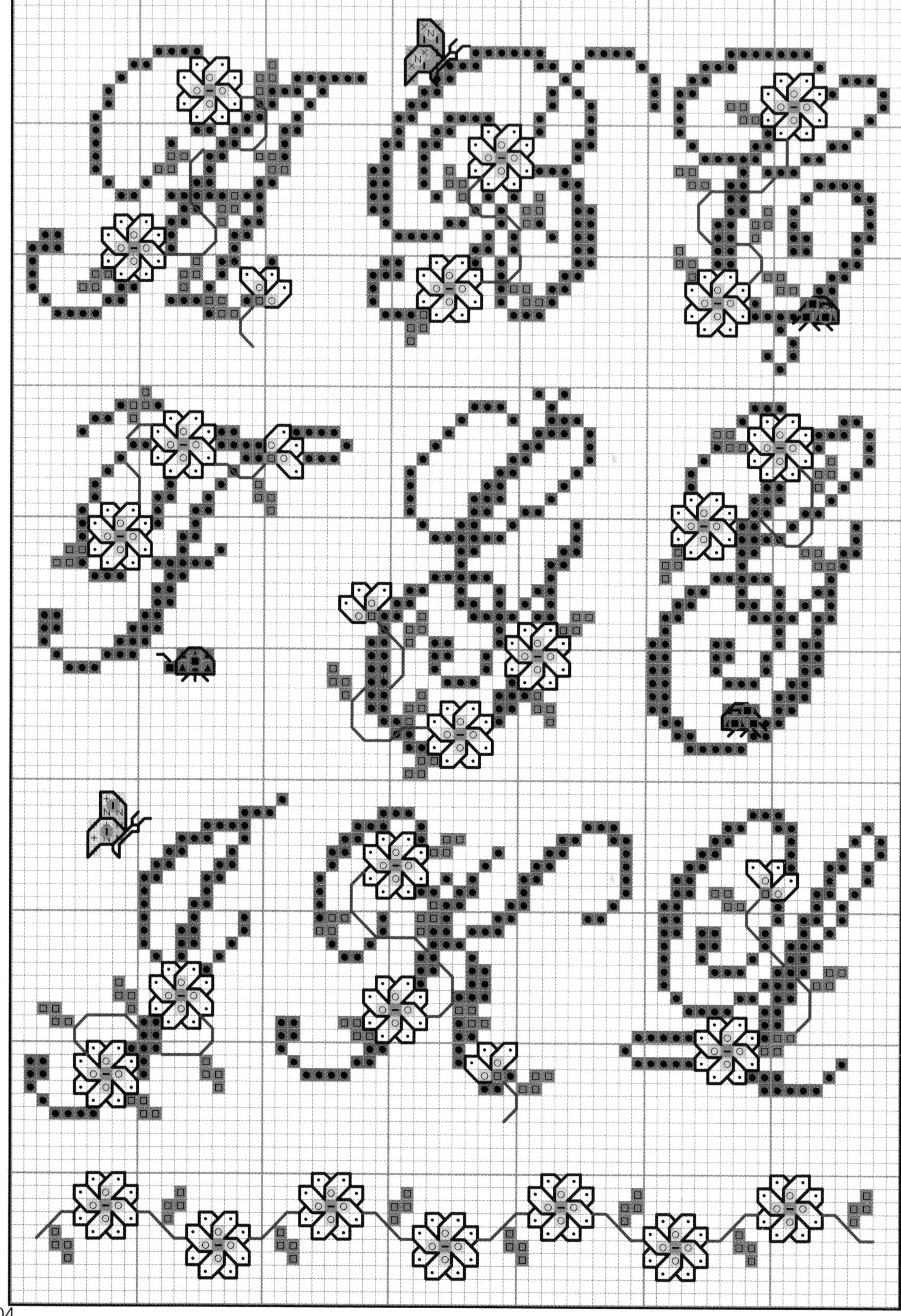

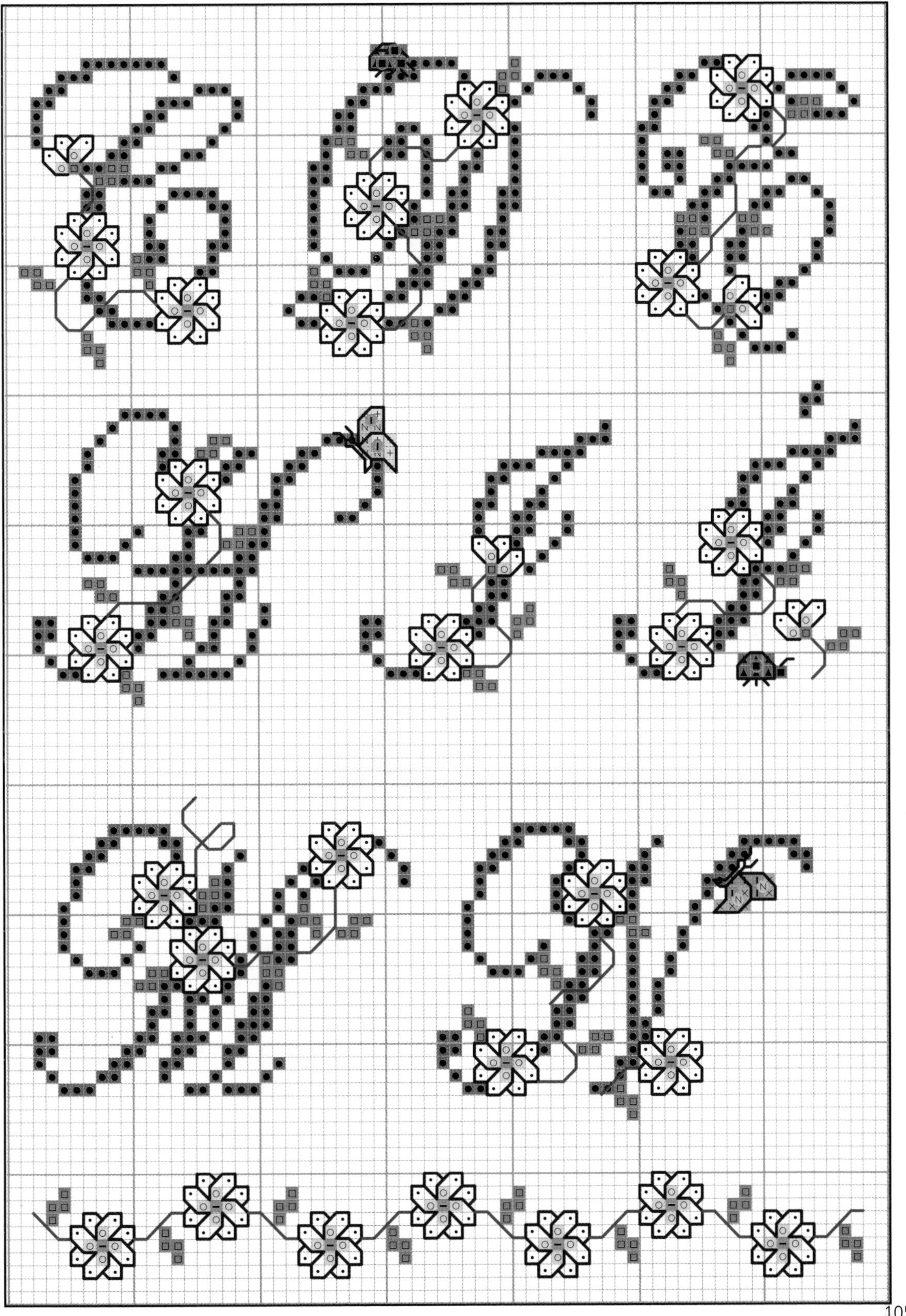

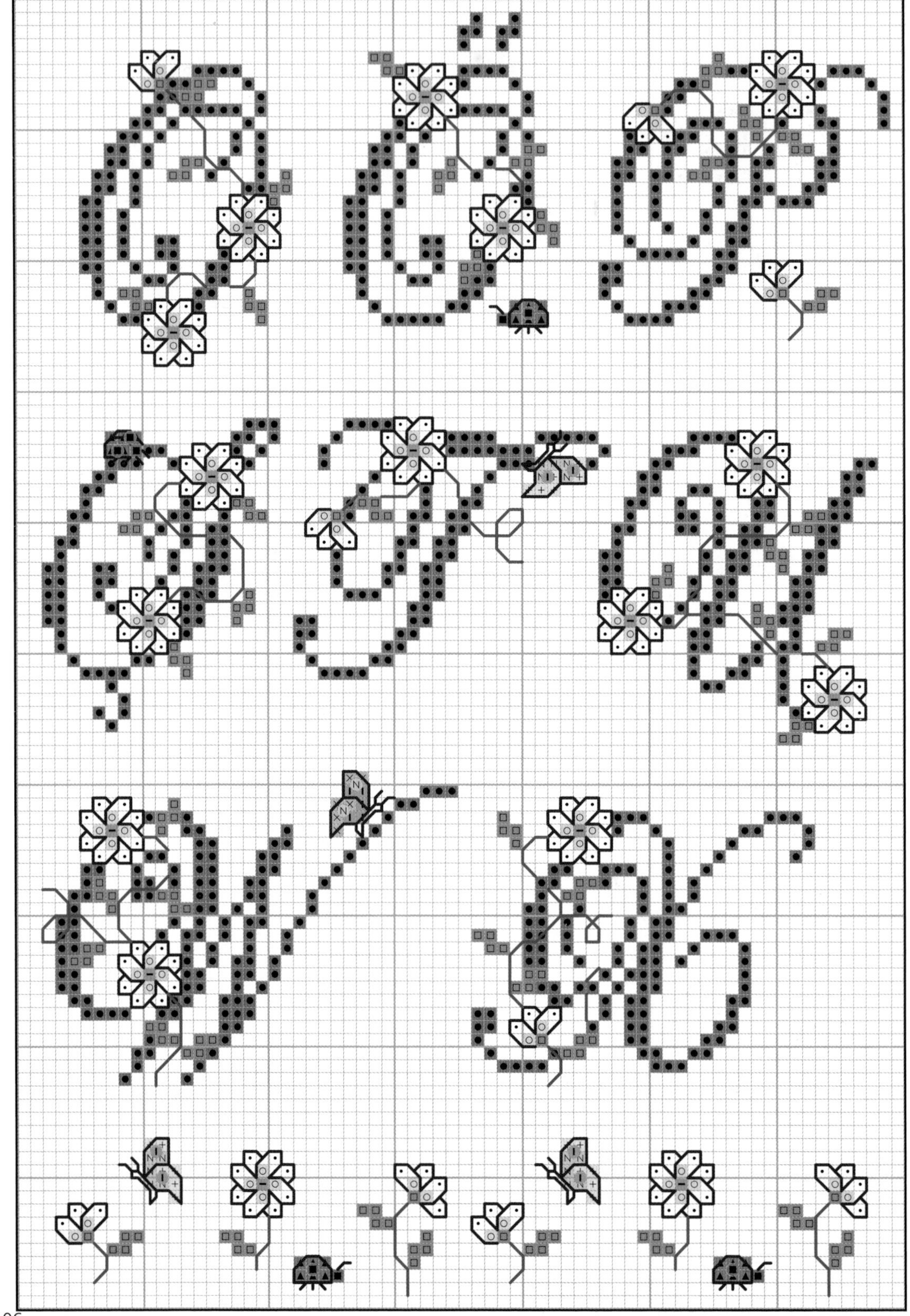

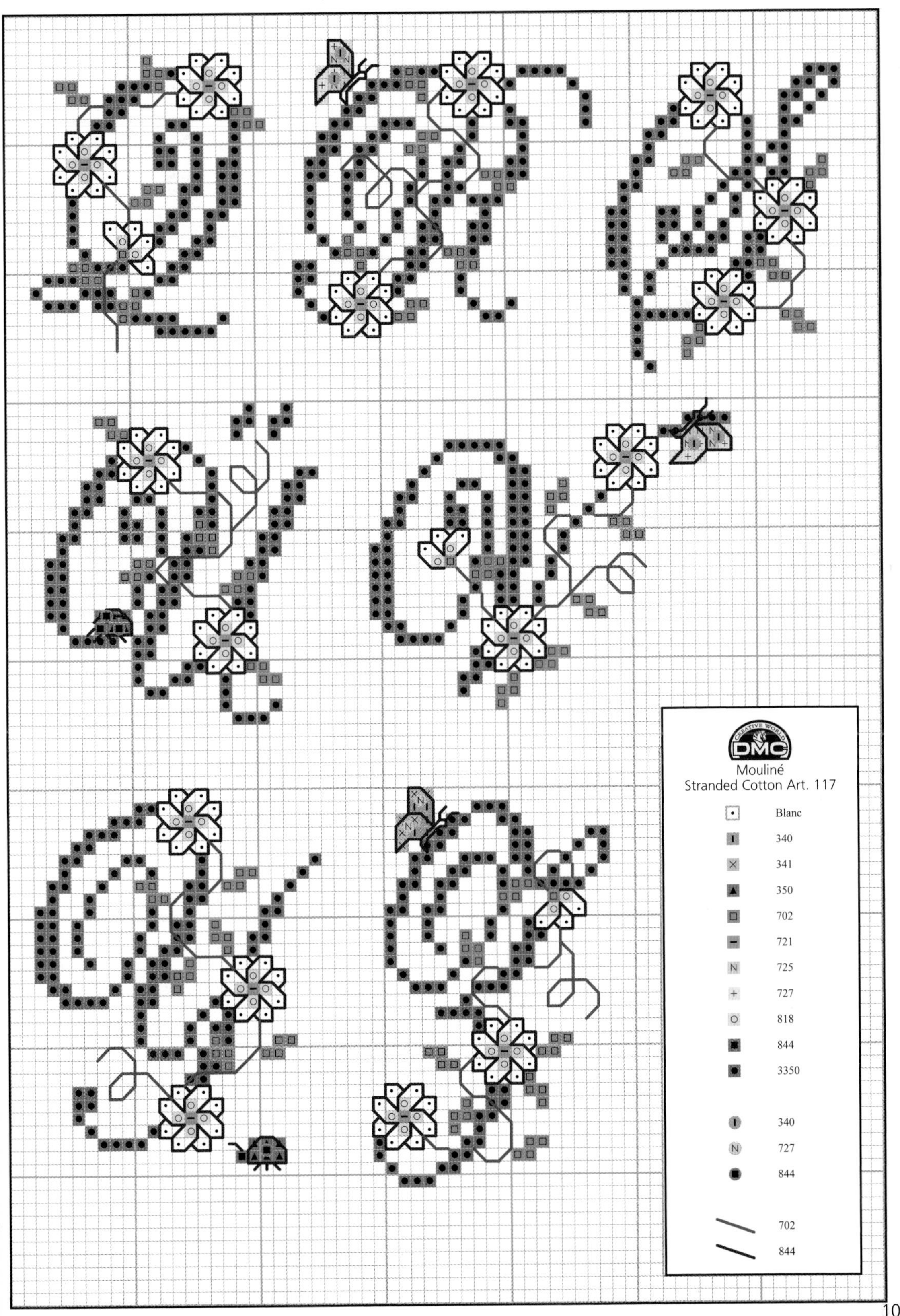

DMC
CREATIVE WORLD
Mouliné
Stranded Cotton Art. 117
Blanc
340
341
350
702
721
725
727
818
844
3350
340
727
844
702
844

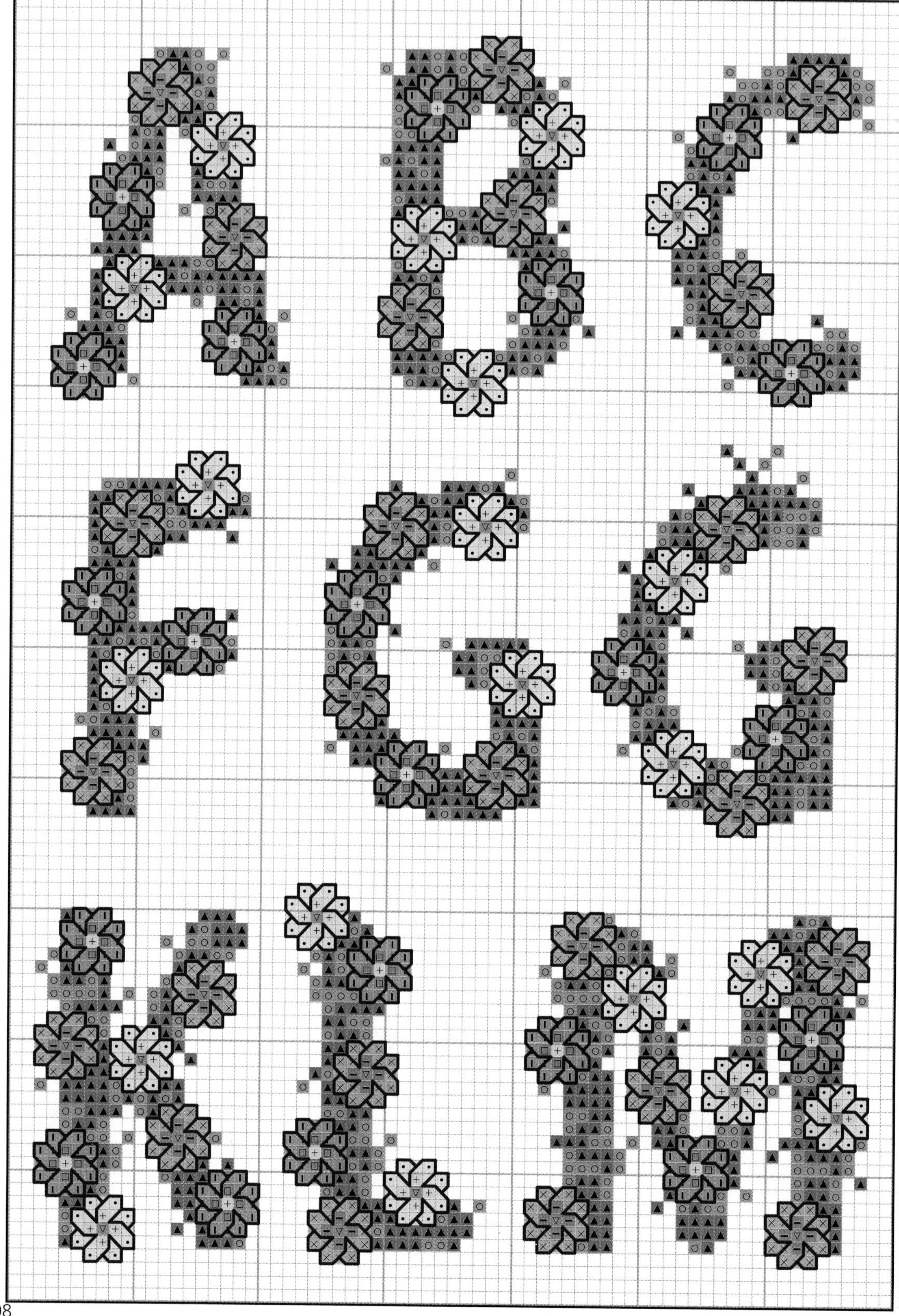

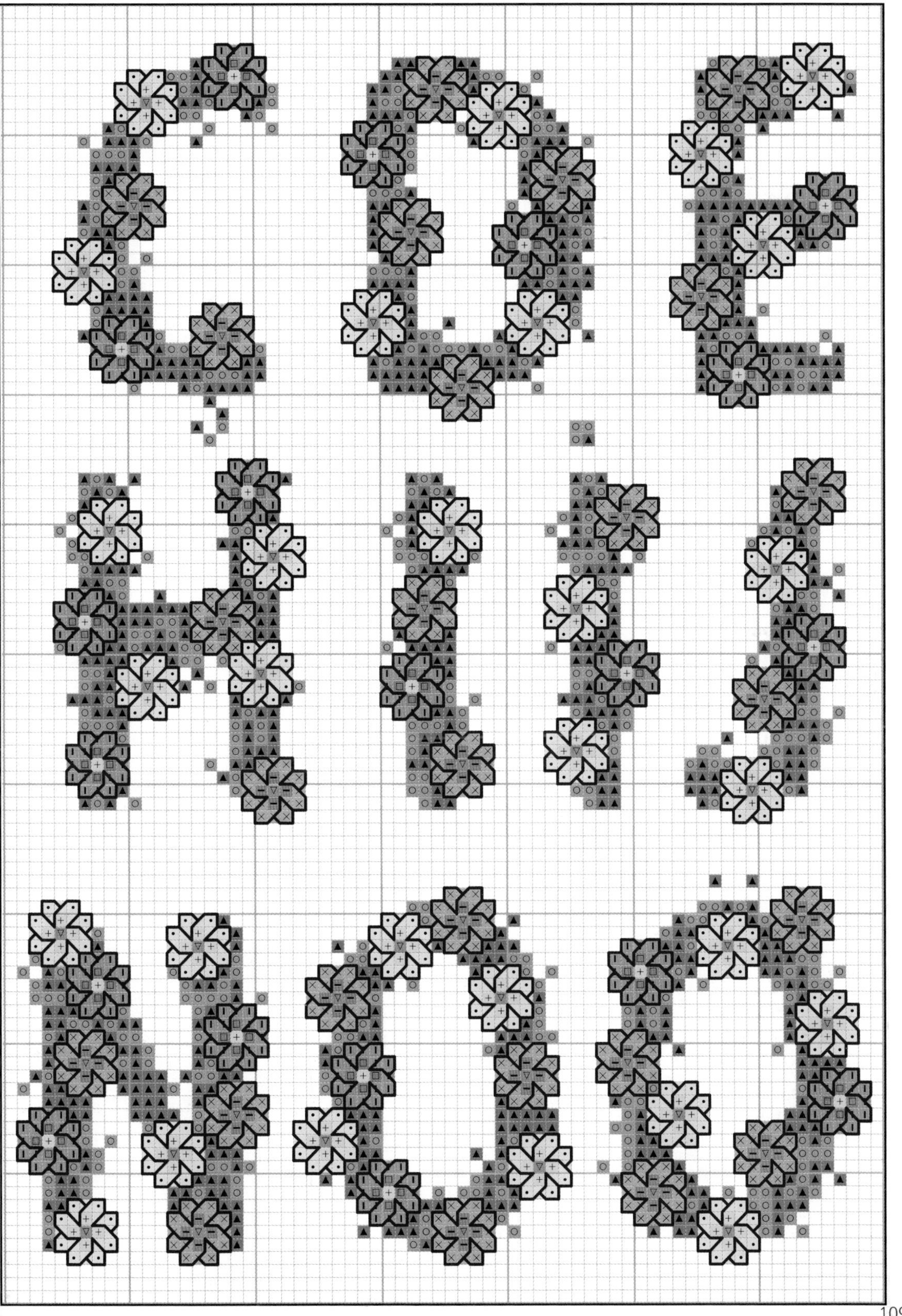

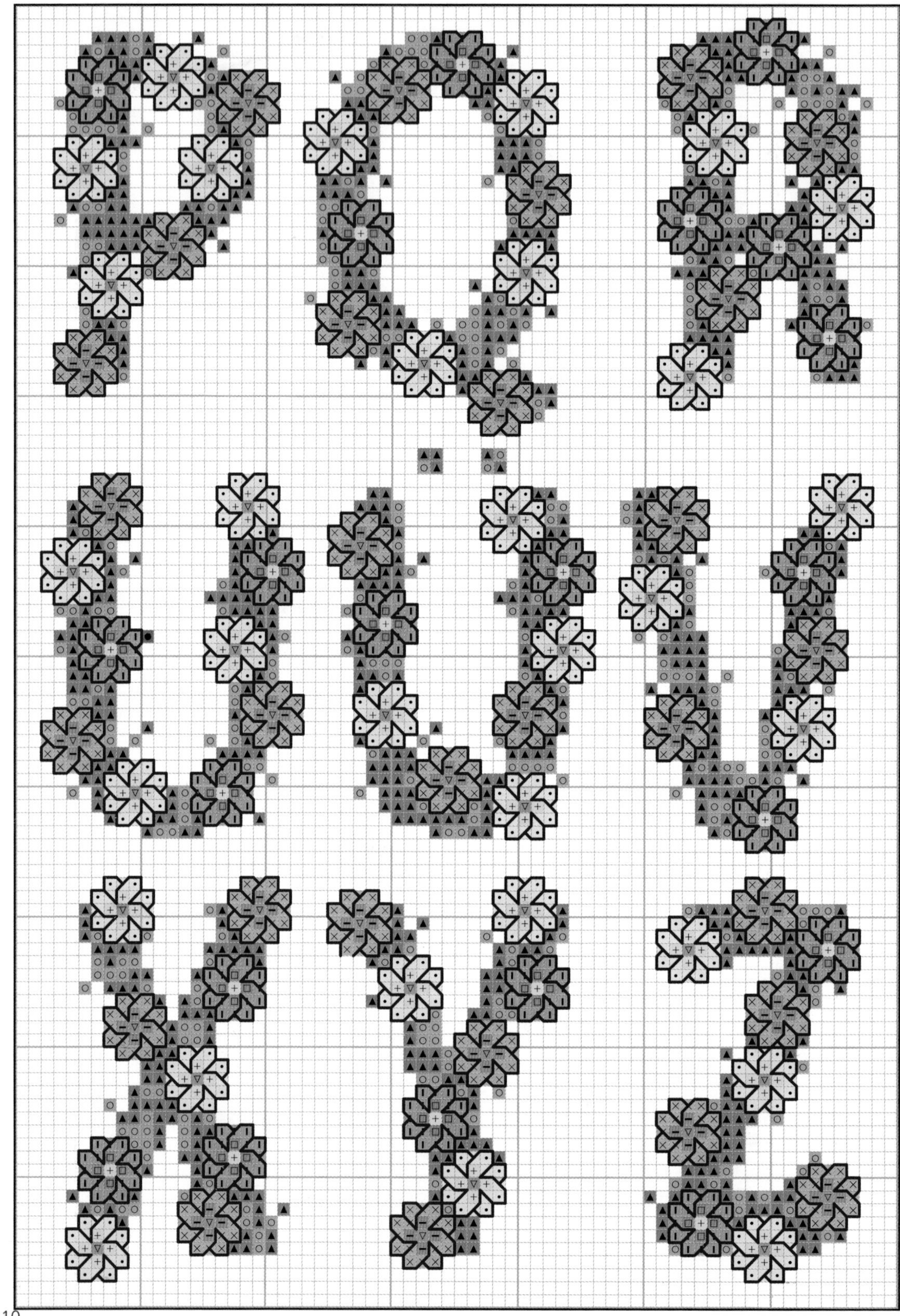

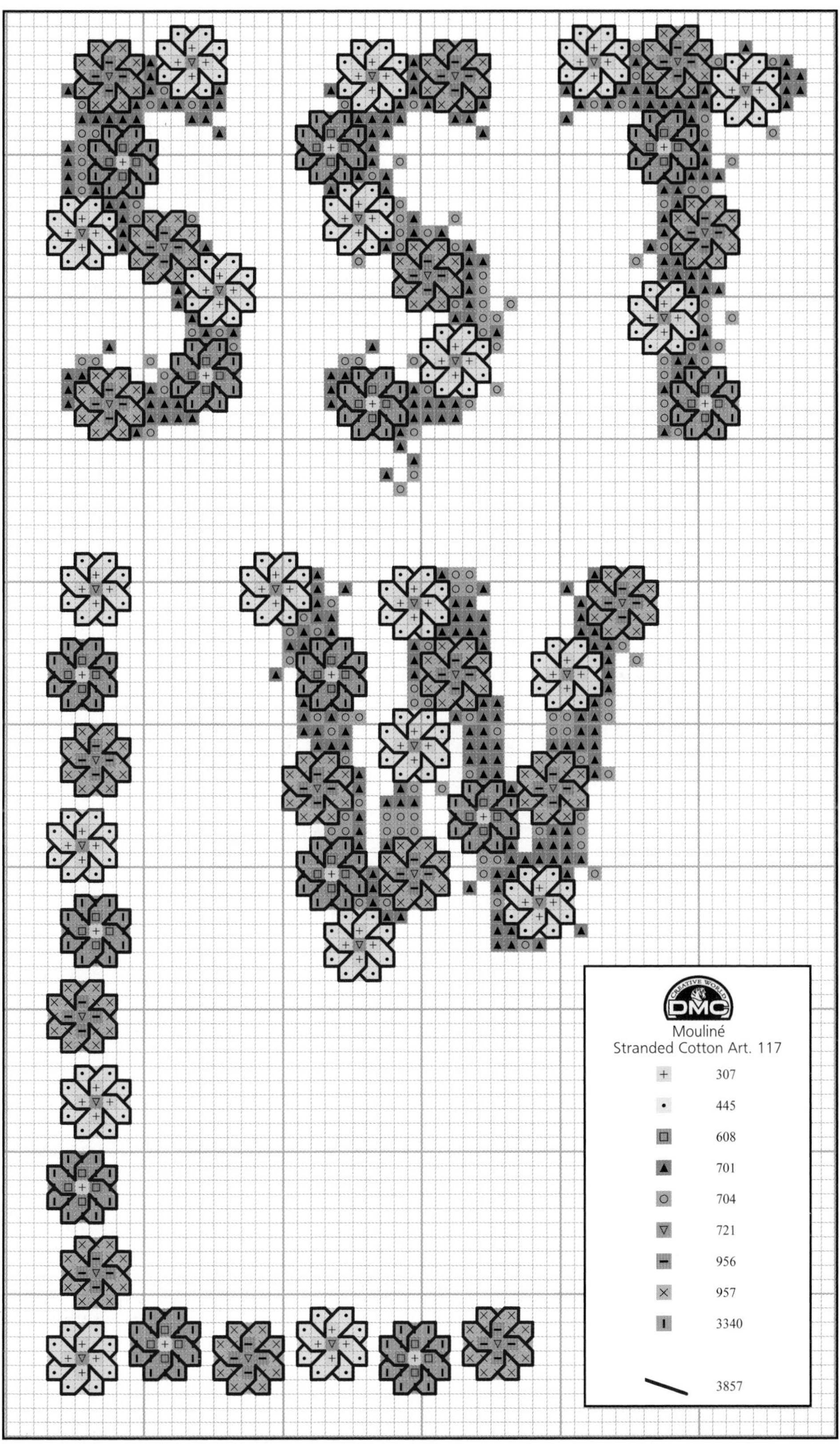
DMC
CREATIVE WORLD
Mouliné
Stranded Cotton Art. 117
307
445
608
701
704
721
956
957
3340
3857